I0022475

openDemocracy Quarterly

The **openDemocracy** Quarterly
Series editor David Hayes

Series 1
Volume 1, January 2007. Europe and Islam
Volume 2, April 2007. Turkey: writers, politics and free speech
Volume 3, August 2007. Europe: visions, realities, futures
Volume 4, January 2008. Undercurrent: life after Katrina

The **openDemocracy** Quarterly is available by subscription. Please
write to od-quarterly@opendemocracy.net for more information.

Undercurrent: life after Katrina

Jim Gabour

Edited by David Hayes

openDemocracy Ltd.
London, England

This book was typeset by Mark Gamar (mgamar@free.fr) and
Tony Curzon Price using LATEX.

ISBN: 978-0-9556775-1-9

About openDemocracy

openDemocracy is the leading independent website on global current affairs—free to read, free to participate, free to the world. . . offering stimulating, critical analysis, promoting dialogue and debate on issues of global importance and linking citizens from around the world.

openDemocracy is committed to human rights and democracy. We aim to ensure that marginalised views and voices are heard. We believe facilitating argument and understanding across geographical boundaries is vital to preventing injustice.

Beyond and behind the headlines

We won't tell you what to think. We offer you a spectrum of ideas, from the people who have lived through the events, from those on the ground making a difference, from scholars with expert knowledge.

Our writers provide you with the background information you need to challenge the politics of any place. Every day, we publish new articles and opinions. . . sign up [1] for our regular emails or subscribe to our RSS feed [2] for constant updates.

A place to reflect—a place to be heard

Through our forums you can challenge our authors, question our visitors, express your views and read those of others. Help shape the world in conversation with other informed and opinionated citizens everywhere.

Become part of our global network. Come to our forums [3] and tell the **openDemocracy** network what you think.

Support **openDemocracy**—Free thinking for the world [4]

Everything on **openDemocracy** is free to read and free to share. It's not free to produce. Your support helps keep us independent and open to all—no matter where they live or what they earn.

Make a donation now [5].

URLS

[1] www.opendemocracy.net/registration6/joinMailList.jsp
[2] www.opendemocracy.net/about/aboutRSS.jsp
[3] www.opendemocracy.net/other_content/aggregation.jsp
[4] www.opendemocracy.net/donate.jsp
[5] www.opendemocracy.net/donate.jsp

Contents

Foreword

Right after Hurricane Katrina I was working on the score for Spike Lee's film *Inside Man*. I was still out of my home in New Orleans and had relocated to my apartment in Los Angeles. Spike graciously came to L.A., rather than having me fly to New York City to work. He walked in the door, and before he even says hello he says, "Man we have to do something to tell the story about those levees, those people." Right then my admiration and respect for him jumped even higher because here he was talking about helping others rather than being concerned about the huge commercial picture we had looming over us with deadlines.

So we dug in to make Spike's *When the Levees Broke*. It was really hard to work on that piece because every time I took a break from working on the film, I had to step out into the reality—I still had to find a way to help my Mom, had to figure out where she was going to stay and how to repair her house, and I had to figure out a way to repair my own house while continuing to work to pay for it. At the same time I was finding family members and friends, and hearing from them all their stories of trials and tribulations, stories of how they were dealing with the aftermath of the hurricane.

When I went to my Mom's place for the first time there was only silence. I stood in front of what was left of that house and there were no birds, no sign of life. The grass and bushes were dead. There was nothing. It was a very eerie feeling to stand in that neighbourhood where normally you would hear lawnmowers and cars, and music on the weekend, people talking—and not to hear anything. In my mind I was coupling that feeling at my Mom's with all the footage from Spike's documentary, all those dead bodies. People struggling to stay on roofs, people fearful, trying to get into the water, people losing loved ones.

It makes you ask the question: "Why did this happen?"

My first reaction was one of anger. At our government, for not doing its job and maintaining the levees. We look to government to protect us.

Having got past that, you start to look for deeper meanings. I was having a conversation with a friend of mine in NY. He told me: "Man, there's a bigger story here. We can't see it now, but there has to be some good that comes out of this." And that's where the title of my album came from: A Tale of God's Will (Requiem for Katrina).

"A Requiem for Katrina"—that part of it came because all of the people who suffered and all of the people who lost their lives. All the pictures of those dead bodies, they haunt me. You want to give them a proper burial, a proper send off. I mean, that's the way we do things in New Orleans, we treat them with respect. When you look at what happened in the City and all through the Gulf region, with the aftermath of Katrina, you see a community of people who carried themselves with great dignity in the face of immense tragedy. They deserve to be remembered and honoured.

It's a moment in time I don't any of us think will ever forget.

For me personally it was filled with mixed emotions, because you look at the news and you say: "OK they're calling us refugees. We're not refugees. They're looking at African-Americans and they're saying these people are looting. At the same time they're looking at white Americans and saying these people are foraging for food."

So in the midst of this horror you were hit again with the certain realisation of people's biases. I don't think this was intentional. I don't think it was malicious. It's just part of who we are as a culture. And it's another wake-up call to the amount of growth we have to do as a society and as a culture to make things better.

So the prayer is for all of that. It's for the folks who suffered, the folks who died, it's for all of us to come together and start to realise what we have to do as a city and as a country and as a world community to make things better.

Right now I think it's an interesting time to be back here, because I feel we are living a pioneer's existence. We are kind of left to our own devices. Like most people around the world know, there's been a slowdown with the government, and with all of that when I drive around to some of the hardest hit areas, I see amazing things. I see people rebuilding their lives on their own, just with the sheer will of having the desire to come home. There are still many people who aren't here, and we have a long long way to go, but I am very proud of my City. I am very proud of what's going on here in terms of what the private citizens are doing.

We have a desire to rebuild our community here, and there has been an extremely large effort to forge ahead, in spite of all the obstacles that have been thrown in front of us. It's an amazing thing. I have seen some clergymen and some business people come together to work as a unit and basically bypass the political process, as they have not seen results from going that route. And frankly, that's what we should have been doing all along, even prior to Katrina. So that's part of the "Tale of God's Will", where there are some great things that are coming about because of this tragedy.

But I don't want to paint the picture like everything is all rosy here, because it's not. We still have a long way to go. We still have to reinforce the levees. In spite of that, just the other day the President struck down a bill that was designed to rebuild those same structures. So here we go again with our very existence being politicised.

We still have those hurdles to overcome.

But that's when the "Requiem" part comes in, where you have to say a prayer.

Despite all of that, in my Mom's neighbourhood, people are coming back. You're hearing the buzzsaws, you're hearing the hammers, and they're going about trying to rebuild their lives.

It's ironic how people get thrown together in times like these. Jim Gabour and I flew back into New Orleans from filming together in Japan, just a few days before Katrina. We were exhausted, still living in another time-zone, fourteen hours out of synch, and suddenly here we both were at our homes, faced with the life-threatening task of making rational decisions about whether to stay or go. Decisions about how to make our homes safe in only a matter of hours. Decisions on how to get our families, our loved ones, to safety. And a couple of years later here we are together again, talking about what we learned from this, an event that turned out to be the greatest tragedy in American history, about how we survived.

And how New Orleans, this great bawdy old town, has survived.

It's our home, you know.

Disarmed

In a return to the putrid nightmare of post-Katrina New Orleans, a hard lesson about what is needed to keep on the right side of life.

In the end I decided not to take it. There were the army roadblocks and checkpoints going into the city, and vehicle searches. I did not savour the prospect of being found by the United States military to be in possession of an unregistered weapon, even if it was a sixty-year-old, second-world-war souvenir and had not been fired in decades.

But I supposed I was more haunted by the idea of giving in, of saying that civilised rules of conduct no longer applied, of asserting that carrying a gun was the only means of survival. I kept running the constantly-repeated video images of looting and lawlessness through my mind, the vicious looks the looters threw at the cameras as they ran by. They could still be there, a nest of them, camping in my home. There could be... there could be anything. I supposed that was when I shook my head and stopped. This was all getting too big in my imagination. I was being a fool, giving in to the Bad Guys. And thus I made up my mind.

I would not take the gun.

It was a decision I would come to regret.

South Louisiana bayou country is a powerful, deep place, and yesterday morning the land made its point softly and without effort. A full harvest moon hung just above the tree line to the west, golden and soft-edged, while at the same time in the east, rising out of a twenty-foot-thick gauzy blanket of fog, a blazing red sun slowly cleared the horizon, the perfect disk intersected by the thin horizontal cuts of low clouds.

As I drove the old bottom-heavy Mercury up onto the elevated highway outside of Lafayette, I could see the cane fields spread out in all directions, green and uniform like a giant's out-of-scale carpet. Only about a quarter of the fields were already blackened and cleared. At harvest time, the quarter-mile green squares are purposely set with a controlled fire to burn off the superfluous lower leaves before the ten-foot-tall stalks are gathered. I remember when I was a child being told to stay away from the autumn fires, as all sorts of animals and snakes rush headlong from the fields, fleeing the smoke and flames.

Which was why, I suppose, there were numerous "Bear Crossing" signs all along the highway as I rode southeast through Terrebonne parish.

I was lulled by the passing scenery, given such comfort by rural memories that I almost forgot why I was riding through the countryside in my mother's huge squeaking car with a trunk full of water, machines and provisions. I was driving into New Orleans, a city first ravaged and then abandoned, to see what parts of our lives had been left intact. And if this narrative has already grown a bit flowery, I suppose it is in reaction to the fact that I was truly frightened, and was looking for anything at all to keep me calm and level-headed going into a place so recently a seat of anarchy and death and all the horrors in between.

OK. I was scared.

The first signs of the hurricane began immediately upon crossing Highway 1, the sole thoroughfare all the way down Bayou LaFourche to the Gulf. We crossed the bridge and came upon a clutch of uprooted river oaks, the first of many roofs and signs we would see that had been draped without care or seeming effort in the remaining trees. Highway 90 had been cleared of debris and limbs. Amazingly so. It had only been three weeks since the Category 5 storm had marched across the coastline, and here was a major highway, running freely and without impediments. The shoulders of the road, though, were piled high with trimmed and stacked limbs, the leaning trees cut off roughly as they approached the roadbed on both sides. The leaves were already dead and brown, and there was a sense that whatever had happened to so severely disrupt, and then hack into submission, the surrounding forest was long gone.

There were few cars on the road, it was early on a Sunday morning after all, though stores and cafes were opening in each of the small towns and villages we passed. Signs of normalcy were everywhere, a Sunday all-you-can-eat crab boil, docks lined with airboats and shrimpers, fishermen just coming back into port at dawn, drinking tall-boys of Budweiser for breakfast while sitting on the bows of their swaying boats.

About half the stalls in the Westwego fish market were open, including our favourite, Amy's, which specialised in blue lake crabs the size of our Mercury's hubcaps.

Along the divided highway more and more mom-and-pop stores coming open, each with progressively more wind damage, but still nothing severe enough to make you instantly think hurricane.

Then suddenly we were up on the Westbank Expressway, only seven miles from the Mississippi and New Orleans. Six lanes wide and we barely see that many cars as we approach the toll booth for the bridge. A rising dread, and dryness in the mouth. And then there is the first reminder of what we are to face. An armed roadblock of national guardsmen and sheriff's deputies set up in the centre of the roadway. They take one look at my elderly car and motion us through, smiles on their faces. "You've no idea where you are going," their faces say.

We continue up the bridge and get off at the first exit on the New Orleans side, Camp Street, headed into the central business district.

Instantly there is a car coming up the street the wrong way, half a block away, headed right at us. He swerves with a squeal, and waves as he passes, sensing rookies coming into the city. I can read his face, too: "Hey, I drive any way and anywhere I want. No rules, here, folks. Better figure it out quick."

Stoplights and signals are dark. Most are twisted round their poles and tilted at diagonals to the ground. There is debris everywhere, but much has been pushed into the gutters. We pass the glass front of the contemporary arts centre, and come to a halt in the middle of the road to get a sense of where we are and what is happening. It is our first bit of legal disobedience, but we need to get a grip. There is no one about, in any direction. The only noise at the moment is the sound of a half-dozen choppers passing quickly overhead.

My stomach lurches, and the physical unease makes me even more unsettled emotionally.

The smell

We drive onto Poydras and turn north, the vast boulevard draped with downed wires, its turn lanes filled with garbage, aluminum cans, plastic bottles, and unidentifiable rotting masses. I don't speculate, just drive by.

The first of the smells enters the car. It is, to speak politely, the faint background smell of sewage. Followed by a stronger scent. Death. I think reflexively: "Something is dead nearby, road kill maybe, an animal caught in traffic." But that is not the case. That smell is never to leave while we are in the city.

We turn right onto O'Keefe, now heading toward Canal and Baronne Street, where Faun's office is located. Another car is coming up the street the wrong way, but turns just before he reaches us. A few blocks further, on the right, many mechanical-looking trucks stand vibrating outside the venerable Fairmont Hotel. There are multiple generators, powering the building, portable air-conditioners blowing fresh air into its halls, and one giant tanker that appears to be pumping the last of the Canal Street water from one of the rare basements of New Orleans beneath the hotel. We pass the truck slowly.

And I experience my first brief moment of terror.

It is the smell of that water. The water we've seen on TV for almost three weeks. It is black and greasy, but it is the smell, the smell that never oozed from my TV 200 miles away, that holds the horror.

Death is below its surface exhaling bubbles from the corruption of flesh, the fermentation of misery. Sour human and animal urine and sweat. Flowing rivers of shit. Rotting food. Poisonous petrol waste.

I smell the bowels of hell. I try to exhale and take nothing further in. I gag. Faun looks like she has stopped breathing, is holding her breath. I speed up and we roll onto Canal Street, turning to the kerb a couple of spaces down.

The smell has dissipated now that we are off the side street. I stop the car and try to regroup.

There was no physical threat from the stench. I know I have never smelled anything that bad in my life, but still it was only a smell. A horrible horrible smell. Evil and yet so real. Once again I saw in my mind the news footage of people up to their chests in that water, wading through miles of it with their children on their backs.

I had passed a small amount of it at a distance, filtered through a car air conditioner. And felt faint.

We are stunned. We need to keep moving, start the car again and turn onto Baronne. At the first stoplight an eighteen-wheeled generator truck is powering up the Pere Marquette Hotel, and on the ground floor Faun's favourite restaurant, Renee Bistrot. Across the intersection, Faun's building, the old First National Bank of Commerce building. Her offices on the 18th floor. We pull over on the opposite side. The lobby doors are partially boarded but one has the top glass door broken out. I climb over, but find the inner doors are locked and no way to get in. Climbing back out over the broken glass proves harder. Faun tries calling some of the building's other occupants on her cell while I walk down the block looking for another way in.

All the buildings are lined with a dark brown horizontal smudge about three feet up their sides, the high-water mark. The smell is muted but fouls every breath.

Up to eighteen

Every shop on the Baronne Street side of the building has been looted. All the glass fronts are broken in. I go in one and another to see if I can get through their back inner doors into the building lobby but the first three are locked. These are stationery stores, copy shops, photo processing drops. There was no food here, just something to steal. The places have been uniformly and violently trashed. There seems to be human faeces everywhere, some beneath pools of residual water. A grey vapour rises a few inches above surrounding pools of flood water.

At the fourth doorway I see that the rear door has also been broken through and there is a way to get inside the office complex.

I call to Faun. We do not hesitate. We can't at this point. Inside, the wide hallways are pitch-black. We stumble over dark objects, but don't look down. We turn on our two battery-operated pocket maglites, and aim them forward. They create small circles of light which we keep just far enough ahead so that we can see where we are going but can't really make out what is beneath our feet. Better that way.

I hear noises.

The Bad Guys. And me armed only with a four-inch-long flashlight. I call out. No answer. No sound now. No turning back. We keep moving, find the elevator lobby, then the staircase. I open the door to an even deeper blanket of darkness, now wrapped in unbearable heat. The stairwell is acting as a chimney. There is a floor below us, below ground, and The Smell is back, amplified by the temperature of the closed stairs. We rush upward, breathing through our mouths and sweating. Sweat that quickly absorbs the smell surrounding us and begins dripping off our clothes.

I feel infected. I keep climbing, keeping just ahead of Faun. More noise above. I am braced for what might be there. I keep climbing, and calling out. No answer. I think of The Pistol. If only I had The Pistol, my heart would not be racing like this.

I truly believe for a moment that I would not be afraid the building was still being looted. I would not be worried that around the next turn of the stairs there would appear one of those twisted faces from the television screen. I wouldn't be afraid.

I would still be afraid. Probably more of myself holding the weapon.

Suddenly, on the next landing there is an air vent and some light. Then at floor five, there is a small square open window. Outside air comes in, and the sickness of the atmosphere begins to lessen.

We are at the eleventh floor when a man in shorts and a t-shirt surprises us by emerging loudly from an open steel door. He carries a computer and several accordion files.

He is exhausted, not threatening, and turns out to be a very young lawyer, as grimy as we, and on his fifth trip of the day carrying his possessions down from eleven. He puts down his burden and sits on the floor, tells us this is his second day of bringing things down, and his legs are giving way. He doesn't want to abandon clients' records and cases, but no one will help him, and he just cannot make one more trip. He estimates it will take him ten more to get the major pieces from his office.

We can't stop, knowing this one trip may be all we have. Up to eighteen.

At twelve we realise that only one of the steel staircase access doors we have seen so far has been open, the door just below us at eleven, where the winded attorney still sits. Faun knows what I am thinking and tells me that even if the door isn't open at eighteen, she has been told that the door to the utility floor at nineteen has been taken off its hinges. We can go up there and descend another internal staircase that does not lock.

Sixteen. My shirt and pants are heavy with sweat and the absorbed scent of the building. I have a mad urge to rip them off and run upwards to escape into the open air. Logic tells me the clothes are protective and that the air above is just as bad as in here. Logic tells me. But I am getting claustrophobic, in the building, the staircase, and my clothing.

Seventeen. The staircase window is open, and the heat lessens again, ever so slightly. I look around every corner as I turn it, hoping the open door will be ahead. I reach the landing at eighteen and there it is. Open. I mount the last flight with more energy and stand looking into the floor of offices with renewed hope.

It is then that I notice Faun standing one landing down, going through her purse.

She looks up at me, her face twisted.

"I don't have my key," she says.

"Your key?"

"The key to my office door. I think I left it in the car."

I lean on the wall and stare ahead. Out of breath. Out of will. It is all I can do to stand there, hoping I am not hearing what I am hearing. I make myself do something.

"I'll kick down the damned door," I say. The cowboy syndrome takes the lead. I am hugely angry, and trying not to be. She has walked up eighteen floors, too. I know she is hurting.

But she maintains her poise. She thinks and moves.

"Let's go see first. It may be open." Faun leads the way.

I follow. I had no idea this was such a huge warren of offices spaces, corridor upon corridor, hot, stuffy, airless. I am lost instantly. Faun stops. Points.

"It's locked," she says.

We are deflated again.

I am a male, and males think in a certain way. We are reinforced to do so by the cultural stereotypes in which we are immersed every day. So the first thing I think is: "It's a glass door." I start looking for the fire extinguisher. I saw this in a movie. A fire extinguisher and a glass door.

"I'll pay for it if they ask," I declare, starting my search for a bettering ram.

Faun has more sense. Puts her hand on my arm.

"They probably have a duplicate key in the office administrator's desk," she says. "Don't do anything until I get back."

I agree and sit on the carpet in the hallway, then quickly get up again. If I rest, if I stop moving forward, I will not be able to regain the energy to get moving again.

I am already physically and emotionally drained. I look at my watch. It is 9:30 in the morning. I look at it again. It is still 9:30.

Faun approaches, her hand in front of her. She holds two keys.

"I think it may be one of these," she tells me, not meeting my eye.

The first key does not work.

She takes another breath and slides the next one in, turns the knob. The door opens.

We look at each other, feeling our lives simultaneously turn another corner. This is all real. Small triumphs in the middle of hell. Small bits of hope being dispensed one at a time. We need to cling to the hope that this will be over. That what we are experiencing will not be the new normal day.

The next half hour we gather and sort only the most necessary files. I have to carry the bulky desktop computer, so everything else must fit in a single box to be carried down the eighteen flights by Faun. The house insurance papers. Deeds, bonds, pending cases. Judgment call after judgment call. We find a couple of bottles of lukewarm water and drink, trying to replace what we are losing. Faun takes what remains and waters the plants that are still alive in her office. I admire this, even while I impatiently pace the room. Here she is, trying to nurture life, knowing we may never be able to get up here again. She is giving them one more chance at making it. What the hell. Great that she can still think that way.

We start down. The staircase is getting hotter as the day progresses. The hurricane has been followed by record heat. We are both sweating freely now, and I am having a hard time holding onto the metal computer CPU. I have to carefully place it on the stair railing and change my grip every few flights. Faun too is stopping frequently. Her glasses keep slipping off her nose and she cannot see without them. Then we hit the dark floors. She cannot hold the box and a flashlight too, so she gets close on my back as I try to balance the computer and aim the small flashlight directly on the stairs at our feet.

We descend two more floors, ever more slowly. It is getting hard to breathe, the heat and smell rising exponentially. I estimate we still have four more floors to go, when a landing door bursts open right in front of us. I almost drop the flashlight. It is an elderly gentleman, on a mission like ours, carrying a small bag. Faun knows him, and his partner. They are developers of historic buildings. He has no flashlight. In return for us leading the way, he takes on Faun's burden and she takes his lighter bag.

We exit the stairwell into the excrement-filled lobby. The man tells us he knows a better way out, a side hallway that leads to an adjoining building lobby for condominiums and a hotel. He tells us there is a security guard there, but it is a bit far from where we have parked. I volunteer to go back through the looted store to the Merc, and tell Faun I will make the block and meet her there.

Walking toward the daylight I can see how completely and senselessly the place has been ransacked. The room's stock, printer ink cartridges, pens, notebooks, have been knocked off shelves, torn and thrown about for sport. Pads ripped apart and used for toilet paper. I hold my breath until I get to the sidewalk.

I place the computer on the back seat gently, like it is some priceless relic from a tomb. I try and clean my shoes before I get in, realising how filthy and wet I am myself. The engine turns over and the air conditioner comes on. I am again temporarily safe. I needlessly squeal the tires taking off around the corner to pick up Faun, then try and calm myself. No need transmitting anxiety like this to someone else.

But there she stands at the kerb, box at her feet, waiting for me. She picks up the box and drops it into the trunk, unperturbed, much more at peace than I can even pretend to be. I decide I need to buck up a bit more.

A deep breath

We cross Canal again and head away from the river. The streetcar lanes are packed with emergency vehicles and army trucks. The outside lanes are solidly filled with generators and air-conditioning trailers, each attached to a different building, sucking out moisture, mold and foul air. Many of the hotels are occupied, with people going in and out onto the sidewalk in droves, mostly emergency workers, soldiers and media. I drive slowly, inspect the faces we pass. They don't seem to care. There are no smiles here, no joking. These are all very different people, from very different walks of life. Joined by the horror. They walk in a sort of controlled stumble, looking straight ahead. Few conversations to be heard over the roar of the machinery. No small talk. Every jaw is set. Every body is stiffened, a fighter awaiting the next blow.

The living are a hard vision. I try to watch individuals as I drive, but they all merge into the same person, a slightly bent figure carrying the weight of these last three weeks, a human burden heavier than can be imagined by those of us who are just now entering the city. I have seen death and dying on television, and groaned in pain. These people have seen it and felt it, smelled it, heard it. They have the taste of death in their mouths. All of them.

They are now a single human, turning over one mossy tombstone after another, looking for life in a graveyard.

We drive two blocks to Burgundy and turn right, heading through the French Quarter to the house on Marigny. The Quarter is empty. There is rubbish everywhere, dead limbs, but little damage and no people.

I had never expected the emptiness to affect me this way. You have heard the term "ghost town" all your life, I am sure. But until you experience the reality of that concept first-hand, especially in a place which you recently inhabited—a place so packed with life and energy— you have no idea what it means. And how that reality physically affects you. I am again tiring of the assault. My brain and body seem to be ricocheting between extremes, and I am trying desperately to find a center, some calm emotional plain from which I can act.

"Breathe deeply," reminds Faun.

This has been our mantra for the last three weeks.

"Breathe deeply." I take the advice, reach far down, and let out a breath through my mouth. Sit there turning the steering wheel, pressing the gas and brake, concentrating on breathing. I continue to drive toward the Marigny.

I am not in New Orleans.

I am in my mother's car.

Neighbourhood

Every step towards life's reassembly is surrounded by risks.

We had spent the evening before in the calm of my brother's pleasant house in the countryside west of Lafayette, deep in the heart of Cajun country. He made us feel at home and unpressured, knowing what we would face the next day. We had even spent an hour and a half at the celebration of *Les Festivals Acadiens*—an extended-community dance party called a fais-do-do, because its guarantees a dancer it will "make to sleep"—celebrating the 250th anniversary of the arrival of the Acadian people in South Louisiana.

The dancers were lively and welcoming, but the heat and the hollow-eyed presence of many other evacuees had not allowed us to enjoy ourselves. Worse, we met a neighbour who lives less than a block from us in the Faubourg Marigny, who was just coming back from a first visit home. Her house had survived the 145-mile-an-hour gales and the rising floodwaters, but looters kicked in her rear door, and had systematically and efficiently carried away everything of the slightest value, even heirloom family photographs whose the frames looked saleable.

She stood on the edge of the dance floor, holding a link of spicy rough boudin in a paper plate while telling her tale, warning us of the possibilities back in the neighbourhood. A band played *L'âche pas la patate* in the background. People were laughing.

She was not, and continued her story, now as a recitation. She relived opening her door, looking into her front room. Even now, a hundred miles away from the house, her eyes moved about the room as she talked.

"After they took everything else, they took its soul", she said. The vandals had taken their time, desecrating every surface and object in her home. "It was my nest", she said, finishing her story with her eyes clouding. She walked away from us without another word or look, and dropped her uneaten food in a trash barrel. She sat at a wooden picnic table a dozen feet away from where we stood, and organised her skirt neatly around her legs. She rested her elbows on the table and stared ahead. Her body began to shake, and she lowered her head and put her face in her hands. I watched for a moment, wanting to reach out and be of comfort, but the tears were already seeping around her raised palms. The flesh of her fingers was whitened with the pressure of a great weight suspended there. I let her be.

I carry that incident with me as the Mercury crosses Elysian Fields Avenue, a block from my own home. Tree damage is everywhere, but the streets have been bulldozed and are passable, and there is no sign of the deadly waters which are still covering 80% of the rest of the city. I feel my foot involuntarily lift from the gas pedal as I approach the right turn onto Marigny street. I have come this far and now find myself timid about what I am to find.

But there it stands. Newly painted purple, and there it stands, sun on its front and draped in shredded banana plants and orange trees. Telephone lines lay tangled in strange wind-tied knots in the street in front of the house, but the electric lines seem intact, and the storm windows are still in place. I pull to the curb a few houses down, and then walk back to make sure that there are no live lines in the wire jumble. I see none, but still use a downed tree limb to move the mess, a ball of wire some eight feet long by three feet high, pushing it into the gutter and away from our driveway and cast-iron fence. Even if the government says that electricity is off-line, I did not come this far to be accidentally electrocuted.

Plus, I seem to have a reduced belief in the pronouncements of our "rescuers" these days.

The lines safely away, we open the gate, walk up the steps and stand at the front door.

I reach into my pocket for my house keys, to find... nothing but loose change and fast-food receipts. They are not in my pocket.

I do not have the keys.

This cannot be happening. This simply cannot be real. Not me, too.

But Louise had been resourceful, and I remember what I had also done two months ago when our housekeeper had locked me out of the house in my pajamas for the second time. I had taped a spare key under the sill of the house. And pushing a still-unbruised sixty-pound bunch of bananas away from the brick piers, I find it, still there and unrusted.

Back to the porch.

Now, the next step. Is there someone inside? What has happened inside?

Once again, I imagine the comfort my fathers pistol would provide at this point, gripped in my hand. But I don't go there and instead begin talking loudly with Louise, banging the door handle and making as much noise as I can. I see her face and know that she knows what I am doing. I keep up the bluster anyway. I am not as brave these days as I was three decades earlier. I have allowed myself to be pacified by the numbing repetitive flow of urban living. Standing in front of this door throws me back into the swampy lowlands south of Bayou Robert, a place and time when hunting a rutting three-hundred-pound feral boar with a slug-loaded twelve-gauge shotgun was a boy's game.

I turn the key nonetheless. And enter.

The front hall is hot and airless, and smells of our cats. But there is nothing amiss. There is no one in the house. Except us. And all is as we left it.

The rooms are odd, though, every item left out of place by us in our fatigued rush to get out of the city in the hours before the roads closed, now a reminder of our state of mind that morning three weeks earlier.

I had just arrived from eight days' shoot in Tokyo and Osaka, my body unsure of its time zone and already nervous, having been chased out of Japan by an approaching typhoon, only to arrive in New Orleans with another less than two days away. Louise had already been living with the storm for almost a week as it slowly and surely rumbled directly toward the city. She knew how stubborn I was about not leaving, not evacuating, ever.

But she knew I was less adamant now. We had jointly rode out an incredibly loud and violent "tropical storm" named Cindy less than a month earlier. The severity of that gale had led me to build new plywood window shutters, stiff sheets that fit snugly inside the century-old cypress frames. After eighteen hours on a ladder and on the roof in high winds putting the shutters in place, I began to listen to the voice of reason, and somehow found myself at 11am Sunday in a VW convertible packed with Louise, the three cats, a bag of food and water and little else.

Seventeen hours later we had arrived at my parents' place, less than two hundred miles to the northwest, shattered and wired. Only to be faced with a direct hit by a second Hurricane Rita, just a few days later. That storm we would ride out with my aging and yet unconcerned parents. Without telling us, my 92-year-old father drove out at the height of the storm to make sure we had enough ice for the beer. He said the raging winds were not a problem, had not blown him off the road. "I just drove with the emergency brake on", he told us with a laugh.

And now we are back home, standing in the same room we had fled, under waves of emotion, such a short time ago.

I go to the back door, and open it, to see if the small cottage out back housing my studio is still in place. It is. Though it holds its place under the weight of two hackberry trees, a forty-foot avocado tree, and a fig-tree. Alongside, down the patio, lay three more fallen hackberries, huge sixty-footers, two from neighbors' yards, crushing all our interior fences. And boxing in the garden shed that holds my generator, axe and dolly.

I decide to tour the rest of the house in the face of what will eventually be massive manual labour. There will be no private tree cutters available for hire in this city for a year. There is a chain saw in the car that I will come to know quite well over the next weeks.

But in the house, all is as we left it, residual nervousness welling from each upturned box and unclosed drawer. Interesting. I can smell us as we were the day of our exit, two different creatures from these that now walk about. But both sets somehow untamed, wild. The memory of civilisation now fading, now arriving back in gentle surges. Half a bottle of a lovely cab sitting corked on the counter with two glasses.

The set of Bach partitas opened on the stereo, the sports section spread about on the coffee table, large headlines boasting yet another set of optimistic articles about the Saints.

Football at this moment rings an internal Pavlovian bell, like cafeteria meatloaf. Crude but comforting, something that truly hits the spot, when digested at the right moment. This is that moment. I salivate for game day.

Take the comfort where you find it.

I do, for a moment only, and then head realistically upstairs to open windows and climb to the attic to inspect for damage. The attic: an error. Necessary, but an error. The wind turbines are missing from the roof gables, and two gaping foot-wide holes sit open at either end of the house. I spend the next hour in hundred degree temperatures, swirls of dust and fiberglass insulation, building makeshift plugs using two second-line umbrellas, tassels still attached, and the better part of as roll of duct tape, to keep out rain until I can do a permanent repair.

I come back downstairs filthy with attic detritus, soaking with sweat, stinking so badly I can smell myself. Black rivulets of sweat run the length of my arms. The front door is open but I don't care. I strip off my t-shirt and pants right in the middle of the room, grab a gallon of bottled water and sit in the cool-to-the-touch clawfoot tub in the downstairs bathroom, pouring the clean liquid over my head and body.

We have running water, but it is oily and holds The Scent. I can't bring myself to have that carry that smell any more than I have to, but I try to conserve the good stuff, and use only half the gallon of clean water. A "military bath", they call it. I towel off and go upstairs to change clothes, realizing at the same time: I have a change of clothes. It's been three weeks. Clothes that I don't have to wash before wearing are a treat.

I pour a glass of water and sit on the porch with Louise, watching the frequent passage of Humvees, electric company trucks, and cops. We are calmer. A breeze carrying the feeblest grains of security has begun to blow. "We live here", I say aloud. No one responds, but I feel better. We live here.

Louise has found her office keys in a side pocket of her bag. With that discovery, I begin to come alive, and realize my house keys are in my own knapsack. Both were within reach when we arrived at our respective locked doors. But they were invisible in the moment.

There have been many moments this day, and we've a couple more to negotiate on our way out.

Alone@Home

*More than half the city is unlivable, and will never be again. I
know now. I've seen it.*

The electricity is erratic, but I am trying to edit the Terence Blanchard
documentary and performance footage I shot in Japan, just before The
Storm. I act like I am working normally, but there is so much to do to
just stay alive here.

Writing about it is hard, and there is no reason to be poetic or find a
more literary way of saying Nothing Will Ever Be the Same.

I am now in residence alone, Louise having temporarily bailed out back
north until the world here calms a bit. She hopes to make another
attempt to reinhabit this Friday. Other than work, I do not intend to
leave again.

Electricity, water and sewerage now function, though spasmodically. I
climbed on the roof to reconnect some wires tangled by a broken gutter
downspout, found some problems, and now have cable and internet.
Supposedly the city will come back and turn gas on house-by-house.
Meanwhile I cook on a propane grill outside the kitchen's back door.
Much like the backyard wood fires in antebellum times. Not romantic
in any case.

There is no mail or regular trash. All phone lines are down in tangled
heaps in the middle of streets.

There is no gasoline at this end of town. A neighbor, needing gas to
escape, siphoned all the gas from my old truck, but he came back by
yesterday to offer to pay for it. No need. I am currently using chainsaw
gas gallon-by-gallon when I have to drive.

There are two supermarkets now open uptown on Tchoupitoulas. About
sixty blocks away. The tiny A&P in the Quarter is finally open 9-5,
but is a madhouse, with little real food to offer. Still I go, looking, by
bicycle to save gas.

The New Orleans police department (NOPD) has become a horrible,
rabid, festering animal. Luckily the national guard remain amazingly
even-tempered, and have been a life-saving defence against our own
cops, keeping the twisted remains of the police department at bay. I
dont know what will happen when the guard leaves us.

Like I don't know who is coming back. More than half the city is
unlivable, and will never be again. I know now. I've seen it.

Daily life, breathing, is eerie and disconcerting. I ate a hot meal at a soup kitchen at Washington Square around the corner last night, from a group of old-time hippies called "The Rainbow Coalition", and felt myself a character walking knee-deep in Steinbeck. These folks from around the country raise their own money, use their own credit cards, and just drove in and started feeding and caring for people.

They have a doctor and a midwife and a big battery-fed boom-box with a great collection of 1960's NOLA R&B. They do not like the Federal Emergency Management Agency (Fema). They got permission from the city to do what they are doing, but the NOPD came to roust the crowd when a brass band walked into the square to play to the hungry people who were eating.

"No permit", they declared, hands on holsters.

Yes: "No permit." Luckily a Humvee of guardsmen showed up just then—the coalition had been feeding them too—and shooed the local cops away.

There are more flies than I ever experienced in the poorest parts of Mexico or India, and mosquitoes who have been feasting on the dead descend in clouds onto your flesh if you stop moving for more than a minute. I wear insect repellent from the moment I wake up until I go to bed at night.

A Fema flier decorated my gate this morning.

I opened it to find a warning to residents in large lettering:

Do not place cadavers or feces on the sidewalk for curbside collection.

A bright yellow dust coats anything non-moving. You can watch it rise from the top of the drying black mud in the streets—the remains of the poisonous floodwaters. Death pollen, everyone calls it.

Corporate carpetbaggers are everywhere. They are taking carriage rides, as tourists, through the Armageddon movie set that is our neighborhood, drinking and raising hell as the mule-pulled carts clop and creak down streets full of rubble. The well-dressed passengers cheer and toast each other, while staring off the carriages at New Orleanians sorting through their possessions.

They are making lots of money off our misery.

The world still literally smells, sometimes in horrible five-minute streams of fetid air that cannot be avoided, and George W Bush is here again for photo ops.

That said, we have community. Seven people and a steady stream of friends and neighbors were over here with two chain saws and wheelbarrows last Saturday to cut and haul out the top of the ten-foot-deep pile of rubble from my patio, only to find the three huge trees at the bottom. Much bigger than we could move.

A man who house-sat during the storm at our neighbor's place said he was looking out their second floor window when he saw a tornado bounce into the middle of our block, snap off the three trees like they were matchsticks and drop them pointing east-west-north, all in less than a few seconds.

It was a mess, but after a day and a half of labor we got all the other rubble to the curb just as a convoy of clean-up bulldozers and dump trucks approached. We gave them water and sandwiches and they worked hard on our block. So by Sunday morning at 10:30am I could walk—with severe limits—in my back yard.

The insurance adjustor came a few hours later, and though he would not discuss the tree in the front, agreed to pay to take out two of the trees in the patio completely—the one straight down the patio and the one from the back—and to pay for the first ten feet—from the root ball to the first big branches—of other. And to get the fence back up, so the cats would be safe. From him I also discovered my policy has a large "hurricane deductible", but I'll be alright.

The expressway off-ramp at Elysian Fields just twelve blocks from the house has almost three dozen boats still tied up there from when it was used as a boat ramp while the water was up. I hope that the neighbourhood hardware stores may open soon, so we can get what we need without having to use gas.

But I found a way to order a fridge on-line from Sears, and have it delivered. They are saying it will be here this week, but who knows. Right now there are thousands upon thousands of duct-taped refrigerators lining every street of the city, each a crisp-edged maggot-covered monument to decay.

That's all I can say for now.

No More Hippie Food! Electricians, Not Lentils!

The refrigerator graffiti tells the story: the margin between survival and submergence is so narrow.

So now we get down to the mechanics of daily existence in the main part of the city, where perhaps 25,000 people now live. Only those 25,000 have returned from the hundreds of thousands who called this hallowed place home pre-storm.

It is All Saints' Day, and the "hippie" Rainbow Coalition are feeding a breakfast to, and clothing, hungry people in Washington Square, a block away from where I write, but the frustrations of trying to exist with intermittent utilities and life-support services is beginning to wear on the nerves of those of us determined to make a go of living back in our homes.

It was cold this past week, and we had been lobbying utilities people to get natural gas turned back on in our neighbourhood, especially since almost all the furnaces in the Marigny are fuelled by gas. For some unknown reason, an inspector had crawled under my house and disconnected the gas line, but one of my neighbours showed me the trick and reconnected us. So we have heat. Now the weather, of course, turns warm. However, the inspectors put padlocks on the lines of any house they suspected had damage, and so those people still have no stoves or heat and now no way to find someone to take the locks off.

Faun celebrated our good fortune and the return of our oven Sunday by baking bread non-stop all day, and after each batch came out, taking warm loaves to our remaining neighbours. She said they smiled and hugged her a lot.

Smaller matters remain obstacles.

The gas cap from my truck was stolen when all the gasoline was siphoned from my tank immediately after Katrina. Again I begrudge no one their escape. But after repeatedly almost suffocating trying to drive my old truck on food and supply runs, I began to also fear an explosion from the fumes.

There are no auto-supply stores open anywhere near this part of the city. So yesterday morning I started the day by becoming a scavenger, driving up and down Elysian Fields Avenue, searching abandoned and trashed cars for a gas cap that would fit my vehicle. On the tenth try I got what I needed. I found immediately that this addition makes for a much easier ride, since I now don't have to drive with my head outside the window.

The old '88 Trooper is on its last legs in any case, having been bashed by flying roof tiles and debris during the storm. The roof is peppered with dents, and the windshield is a spider-web of cracks. If I hit one more good-sized pothole, it will fall into my lap, so I drive carefully.

But the whole frame vibrates badly, even at thirty-five miles-per-hour, from the damage of frequent encounters with quickly-eroding streets. I decide that part of this is due to a serious lack of pressure in the tyres. So after getting my second-hand gas cap, I try to find a gas station with air.

No luck. Every single station, of those few that were open, had had their vacuums and air-pumps broken open and looted of quarters. So I return home to resort to a very, very old bicycle-pump, and with a bit of arm pain and the bashing of knuckles return the tyres to a slightly more circular shape.

The third task of the day follows. Somewhat filled with air and gas and water, the truck and I make it out the ten miles to a large hardware store in the suburbs, transporting home needed roof tin—massive trees had damaged the shed in the patio—plus I need shingle-flashing and window-caulk to reseal the main house, and copper-tubing for the new fridge.

The drive is not pleasant. I drive Tulane Avenue and then Airline Highway from their origins by the main library downtown, almost eighty blocks across Claiborne and Carrolton Avenue, and see no sign of life. Water lines rising as I pass to the west. Not a house habitable, not a business without massive damage and looting, for mile after mile.

And, apart from the LSU Medical Center and the civil district court-house, not a sign of anyone even attempting to get it back together. Not a single soul. No one.

Coming back with my purchases through another part of Central City, on Louisiana Avenue through even poorer neighbourhoods, I see pockets of residents gutting their houses. The water lines, here black, dense, and a foot wide, mark most of these frame structures above the doors of their raised porches, at nine feet. Not deep enough to drown anyone in the attic, but quite sufficient to completely destroy and defile everything inside.

But there they are, undoubtedly homeowners rather than renters, trying to salvage what is left. Which in the best of cases, is only the frame and rafters. The decayed gelatinous contents of each house is now a shapeless mass on the sidewalk. Twice I saw an individual standing in the street, staring at such a pile. Just staring.

There obviously is no sense trying to get anything out of what had been the physical structure of their lives until 29 August 2005. Everything is now reduced to this unidentifiable grey liquid. Formless. Functionless. A blurred picture, a favourite chair, an expensive rug, all part of the same mass.

Personal lives and possessions, melted into waste and set out on the street for anyone to see.

Up ahead shuffles an elderly man in dishevelled and filth-stained clothing, working on his house just north of Claiborne Avenue. He has no facemask or rubber gloves. No haz-mat suit. As I come up alongside him, he pushes another wheelbarrow full of muck onto the pile and pauses to catch his breath. I couldn't help but watch him as I wait for one of the few functioning traffic-lights in the neighbourhood.

He did not look up as he dumps the barrow. I saw his face. It is deep, deep, *deep* in another place. I do not exist there. He continues to look down, started to reach for something he saw, but then realises it was not worth it.

He stands up straight, lets go the handles of the wheelbarrow and let his hands drop to his sides.

"My life come to this."

I could hear it. Unspoken, but there it is, the words hovering, taunting him, darting about his head in unspeakably sour and rancid air.

His emotion, that of the whole neighbourhood, an infinitely magnified gravity, pulling at me, pulling me down, ripping my gut as I drive off, leaving him at the curb.

He is me, but for fate.

I am only a *witness* to this man's pain. I am not living it. I still have my home. I have heat and a stove. Which makes his heartbreak, an old man struggling to find any normalcy at all for his remaining years, by restoring the only thing left to him, even harder to bear.

I drive home, the increasing dysfunction of the truck helping me temporarily to forget.

I block the vision of the Central City with manual labour. After four hours of work, I secure a new roof on the shed that protects my tools and chainsaw and generator. Shortly after sundown, the first rain in two months begins. There are maskers out in the Marigny for the night, for Halloween, but I cannot bring myself to leave the house. I wonder where, or if, the old man sleeps.

I find none myself. Through a long night I am haunted and hurt and at times breathless from rising panic, at the memory of what is just another day in New Orleans.

And I am the lucky one.

A deep-fat new year

The return of fast food: normalcy and warning.

New Orleanians have come to long for, and relish, the mundane. I happily maintain myself as an example of such aesthetics. So the new year is to be a day spent sleeping through rented movies. It takes a long, long drive to the suburbs to find a rental place, and by the time I get there none of the movies that remained in the store were actually B choices, or even Cs. Consequently, I am facing a very eclectic mix of Japanese Zen sword dramas and black and white 1950s detective flicks. I anticipate competing for reasonable couch space with the three sprawled cats who couldn't care less that I am the guy who works for their food.

In spite of this inherent inertia, I go early to visit a friend's traditional 1 January black-eyed-peas-and-greens-and-cornbread meal this afternoon. I guess it's just southerners who must have this menu fed to them annually to magnify chances of good fortune, and I suppose the ritual seems more relevant having lived through this past year, but me, I just happen to like simple home-style food, no matter the occasion.

However, I probably wouldn't leave my comfort zone for the chow and camaraderie. I go for the transport.

I have a new vehicle. The old truck, battered and beaten by Katrina and damaged by gasoline poachers, finally gave up the ghost two weeks ago, and I began the search for a car, a necessary evil, even though I admit to hating driving.

The process was complicated by the fact that there are few unflooded, unspoiled used cars for sale here, but after a week of second-hand negotiations with the nephew of an elderly Cajun gentlewoman in Lafayette, Louisiana, I now am the proud owner of a vintage Mercedes 420SEL.

There was mojo involved, as always, a sort of reverse exorcism, as post-sale I had to remove the sweet but devout lady's many religious medals from the vehicle, especially the large silver crucifix on the visor that was embossed with the two-inch-high message: "The driver of this car is a Catholic. In case of an accident, summon a priest." I rather liked the eeriness of that invocation, so when I removed the piece, I installed it on the top shelf of my mojo altar in the house. My mother would pitch a fit if she knew.

But medals were only part of the automobile karma. There were Knights-of-Columbus floral sachets in all the car pockets, each packet certified to have been blessed and sprinkled with holy water at St Francis of Assisi church. To ensure simultaneous protection from bad odours and bad vibes, I am sure.

I actually thought I had cleansed the car, and was preparing to crank the stereo with Sonny Landreth's slide-guitar, when out came the previously-installed CD: *The Hymns of Medjugorge.* No kidding. A south Louisiana matron finding inspiration in eastern-European tourism miracles.

The car is now purged, though there is a lingering scent of doilies and frankincense.

So it's new year's day, and I am travelling cross-town for a meal because I have only driven the new old car three times, and I figured this is a good excuse to play with the toy. Men are so predictable.

My friend lives uptown. I could go north twelve blocks and travel that direction quickly on Claiborne Avenue, which cuts across the top of the bend in the river, but the journey up there is too depressing. Every home and business on every block of that major thoroughfare from St Bernard Parish on the south to Jefferson Parish upriver is badly damaged or destroyed. The coffee stains from the flood levels go on for miles.

I decide on St Charles Avenue. The trees are beat-up and the streetcar lines are down, but otherwise the beautiful avenue is relatively unscathed. Relatively.

It is in the first blocks of St Charles past Lee Circle that I hit the gridlock. And I mean a complete traffic standstill. On a quiet holiday, with the town deserted.

I get out of my car and walk up half a block to see what the matter is. A massive fender-bender? A stalled Federal Emergency Management Agency garbage-truck? Another loose mental patient? Another streetside suicide?

No.

I find on the next corner a source of the disruption that is far worse and more life-threatening than I had feared.

The return of fast food to New Orleans.

For the last four months, this neophyte village has been eating via a small, very limited food supply. There are only two supermarkets and two small mom-and-pop grocery stores available to feed the entire city. There are a dozen or more amazing restaurants reopened and serving the hungry masses lovingly. So the city the national health surveys have mockingly dubbed "the land of the obese" has been a very healthy place, menu-wise, since the Big K.

But now, today, there they are, on corners directly opposite each other: burgers and fried chicken.

The inevitable return to bad diets—a Wendy's and a Popeye's. Four months after the 'cane, and here is the only fast food in the city, concentrated in one place. A two-block-long line of cars waits for Wendy's Drive-Thru Window. People are cursing and gesturing as they grow impatient for their bag o' burgers. You can't get near the front doors for the crowds, especially at Popeye's, and the line there spills into the right lane of traffic. The chain of spicy-battered bird parts started here in New Orleans, Louisiana, and has its most fanatic hardcore fans here.

The line of people waiting for food more resembles a queue outside a methadone clinic than a fast-food outlet, though I suppose lard withdrawal can be quite painful.

Worse, as I drive onto a side street to get around the unmoving traffic, I get a whiff of what is cooking inside, and feel my own soul groan in hunger.

I find myself drooling on the steering wheel of my new old car.

And somehow feel a notch closer to normalcy. Starting 2006 on a positive note.

Now if I can just get me that #3 spicy dark dinner with a side of red beans and a jalapeno pepper.

Today's vital statistic, Mr President

Amid the murk, a few surprises.

Things are still unworldly and off-kilter here in the bourbon-splashed floodplain. No matter what figures the government throws out, we're still a very small band of settlers, and we're nervous and stressed.

A percentage of the university community is back this week and the next, but many of them, staff and students, are living in trailers in Kenner in Jefferson parish, remote from the city centre. And the community colleges, which were primarily made up of working-class locals, have been decimated.

Delgado had 90% of the buildings on its City Park campus severely damaged, and many of the classroom structures are no longer habitable. That one school is expecting to return fewer than 7,000 undergraduates out of a pre-K population of almost 18,000, and since the majority of its students originated in the now completely defunct New Orleans school system, the college's future is not bright.

None of the folk in charge seems to be able to decide our fate, at least while anyone is looking. They're waiting to do the deals when the shadows move in and attention is elsewhere. Which may mean that action is on the way, since the world seems to have forgotten New Orleans and moved on to other things—or at least they've decided that things aren't so dire here, especially in light of ongoing earthquakes, floods and Senate votes.

Bush flies in once every twelve weeks or so and gets his picture taken by wreckage. He's back this afternoon. None of us have been invited to see him. As a matter of fact the feds have brought back a renewed military presence for the day, ostensibly for the photo op, but more likely because they are afraid that an irate New Orleanian might fling seafood gumbo at the all-powerful president of the United States.

The word is that he gets rashes upon contact with spicy food or ungrateful disaster victims.

Meanwhile the real and living residents hang about, treading water and hoping for regular mail and garbage service. Or phones, or electricity. Or supermarkets and drugstores. Or hamburgers and fries. Or real medical service.

It's odd, though. A few unexpected positives jump out of the muck to surprise you, or horrify you almost every day.

Like this Monday.

On Monday I discovered real and physical proof that most of the Bad Guys (most) are gone.

For the last decade, New Orleans has been under siege by hoodlums and drug gangs, and every third person in the neighbourhood has had their house burgled, or been carjacked, mugged or robbed at gunpoint in recent years including Faun and my good friend TR and six other neighbours.

In spite of a slightly lower murder rate.

My theory is that we had fewer murders not because of less criminal activity, but because the city had found the economic and social circumstances to invent an even less intelligent brand of thug.

The shooters weren't less violent. They were simply worse marksmen.

On this day, I was in the company of a waiter friend from Royal Street who had cut his hand and needed minor stitches. He called and said he couldn't drive himself down to the medical site for treatment because he needed to keep pressure on the wound, which though minor, was messy.

I drove to the temporary Charity Hospital emergency room, set up inside the Convention Center, and parked directly outside. There were few cars and no foot traffic. The ghosts from the nightly news still walk the streets there, but the building is now shining, clean and empty. Except for the emergency room.

This facility is mostly sheltered inside sterile tents, which are themselves inside the huge convention rooms. It is run by former staffers now. The military medics are just about all gone home.

Service is quick and efficient. My injured bud is quite content to be getting delicately sewed up by a sympathetic and lovely young female internist, and I let him be. Watching the stitching of human flesh is not a preferred entertainment for me, even in the strangest of times, which these are.

I wander toward the entrance to the great hall where there are some chairs and small tables set up in a loose grouping. There isn't much going on, and I am a bit spooked, so I strike up a conversation with the one other person in the place. He also seems at loose ends, and is sitting in the makeshift waiting-room reading the morning paper, drinking coffee and hanging out.

I say hello and offer my name and place of residence, and the slightly older gentleman identifies himself as a long-time Charity doctor.

I remark on how quiet it is in the cavernous hall, the smallest sound echoing endlessly.

And this doc says: "Yes, there aren't really that many people here now, compared to before, and not nearly the sorts and numbers of people we were treating in the trauma centre at Big Charity on Tulane Avenue. It's been a very dramatic change."

"Pre-Katrina," he continues after a pause to consider his own words, "I was personally treating fourteen to sixteen gunshot wounds a night."

I must have a doubting look on my face because he repeats himself: "Yes, that many *a night*. The majority didn't die, they just got treated and went right back out there. And you know, I have yet to see the first bullet wound since the storm."

I consider the revelation now. And its implications.

Maybe that fact would give the day-tourist Bush a little less worry.

Somebody ought to send it along to him.

I can picture the commander-in-chief chatting up his aides, wanting to take credit for the statistic in his next press conference. A good spin, it will be, at least on the surface. Which is where he dwells.

Then all of us here in New Orleans can watch George W Bush on the news: an uncomfortable, artificial-looking human male, clad in a $5,000 designer suit, reading in broken, contrived English off a piece of gilded stationery embossed with his name.

He will be easily recognised as a man supremely happy to be back in the safety and comfort of his White House easy chair,

a man

finally and surprisingly

distanced

from

at least

one source of numbers

detailing the circumstances

and frequency

of

death.

Boils next time

The quality of life is getting worse, not better.

By the time you read this, these words will have been edited, proofed, turned into ones and zeroes, spellchecked again. And quite possibly in the process have become quite readable. Unlike many of my other missives, written in passion and the haste to get them out of my system, which I e'd into the world without a second thought. Only a sigh of relief, to be rid of them.

But this time I am writing with pen to paper, and though it is rather a foreign process, it is allowing me to vent once again, and thus, retain my sanity, even while living full-time in my home.

In New Orleans.

Did I mention that I am writing by the light of a solitary lamp powered by the gasoline-fuelled electrical generator outside? A device which also allows both my neighbour's and my own refrigerator to keep working?

Yes.

The generator is noisy, but it does allow me the comfort of knowing that my freezer and refrigerator full of food will not spoil immediately. These days, we have to stock up with large quantities of foodstuffs when we make the long trek crosstown to the sole supermarket. It is quite an expedition, and not taken lightly.

Today's was your standard start to a Saturday morning in New Orleans. Get up, turn on the lights, and discover that there are none. Along with no heat. These power interruptions are such a regular occurrence that I no longer take the trouble to set electric clocks, in the house or my office. I consequently live in a neo-modern world, each room of which is festooned with sets of blinking numbers.

Luckily this morning I still have my backup coffee-maker, an old Cajun four-piece four-cup pot which I have lovingly possessed for over thirty years. I haul it down, boil water—gas stoves are a necessity here—and head out to find a newspaper.

Who knows, Bush may have been here again.

But as I approach the front door I hear a siren, then another. And another, and another. It was only yesterday that the venerable Coliseum Theatre burned to the ground, aided by high winds and low water-pressure. Even with helicopters working in tandem, hauling 800-gallon bags of water from the river to dump on the fire, the theatre burned and disappeared from the earth quickly and finally.

Another bit of our soul gone.

So when I open the door to my home and walk into a wall of smoke and an audio cascade of even more approaching sirens, I become more than a touch uneasy.

There sound to be dozens of fire-engines approaching closely, and as the smoke clears in a breeze, I see that there are. Dozens. I see them wheeling into the neighbourhood, one-by-one, roaring up at the end of my street, dropping into a rubber-burning screaming halt just two blocks north.

Less than a minute later, the deafening thud of approaching helicopters makes me duck. They are flying really low, less than a hundred feet up, and they are carrying the same bags I'd heard were used at the Coliseum. Each of the aircraft is hauling a large round orange sack, suspended from its belly at the end of a long tether. A spray of water is blowing from the upper mouth of each bag as it moves into position, again just to the north of me, and prepares to drop its water.

There is most certainly a fire. Nearby.

I throw on an old warm-up jacket, hop on my bike, and sprint up the street, which is rapidly filling with people in their pyjamas and robes. Two blocks away, just above Rampart Street, people are stumbling into the mouth of a rock-strewn driveway on the eastern side of the street. There is a large open space in the centre of the block and it is directly behind the fires, which are now coming from the upper stories and roofs of at least three buildings. The row of century-old shotgun houses face Mandeville Street, the next parallel street east, but the rear of the burning houses intrude well into the block very near Marigny Street. My street.

Luckily, for me at least, the wind is coming strongly out of the north-northwest, and is blowing the flames straight down the block. *Un*luckily for the rest of the houses on that side of the street. The fire is literally leaping from wall to wall. I can see flames blowing horizontally from the upper windows of one house like a blowtorch, directly into the shattered windows of the next, and then out the other side of the second house.

There must now be at least a hundred firefighters on the scene, and more arriving by the minute. They do not look like actors in a movie.

They look like tired old men, just awakened from sleep. Which is exactly what they are.

I spot half a dozen of them standing precariously on the roof of one house, fully equipped with oxygen-bottles and grappling gear, hacking at the side of the adjoining building, flames just a few feet away and coming closer every time the wind slackens. I lose sight of the firemen as another 800 gallons of water falls directly on them from the sky.

"These guys really *are* heroes," is all I can think. Trite. Simplistic. But, Christ, just *look* at those guys!

People all around me are standing about in clusters with their mouths open, watching the firefighters risk their lives for someone else's property. We start into conscious life only occasionally, each time to simultaneously point at yet another burst or explosion. I can see the faces around me. Neighbours, all wondering if this fire in a gale wind can be stopped before it jumps the next street south and moves into that block. And on into mine.

Thinking this, I pedal one block in that direction, where the fire is headed. The firemen from three trucks have formed their vehicles into a line down the street, directly in the path of the fire. They have of course thought of the same possibility that I imagined. The smoke is blowing directly in their faces, and the heat is already so intense that I have to stay half a block away and watch them stand there, feet set and hoses in hand. Knowing that they have only the small amount of water stored in their trucks with which to stop the flames.

They can see by its short arc, that there is barely enough water pressure to maintain the hose on the giant crane to the north. Not enough for the pumper trucks to tap into the neighbourhood fire hydrants.

It is that way all over the city. Thus the choppers have been brought into use. These men know that, if the 500 gallons they each have is not enough to stop the fire's advance, they will have to evacuate quickly, very quickly. The drivers are in fact already in place in each truck, waiting.

The helicopters are now in a rhythm, dropping a load of water every ninety seconds. I know this because the gentleman standing next to me is timing them. They are remarkable. We are all in awe of the pilots, getting so close to the fires, and we now see them so frequently that we have come to note their individual characteristics. The red-and-blue chopper gets much, much closer to the flames before dumping, but even so, the orange flyer is more accurate, in spite of the rising wind.

One of the bystanders says he heard that the fire was started in the storm-ruined furniture store on the corner, by squatters. Once out of control the wind took it to the house immediately behind it, then the next. And the next. By the time I get near enough to see for myself, the fire is consuming its seventh building. Only two are left between it and the fireline at the street.

That is when the tanker trucks arrive, three at a time.

The pumper-drivers scramble to hook up to the additional water and begin to spray, into the wind. Finally, the additional water coming from the south begins to slow the fire's progress.

And then it is out. The fire is out. We are left staring at three-quarters of a block filled with charred blackened totems.

The houses in this neighbourhood are either made entirely of old-cut cypress or of stucco set on cypress beams. Cypress wood is wonderfully resistant to water. And equally susceptible to fire.

The owner of the last house to burn, a gorgeous two-storey Greek-revival mansion, had just completed hurricane restoration on his home last week.

The water here now has no pressure and lots of smell. It stinks with chlorine. Friends have told me that you can bleach clothes clean by leaving them overnight in a tub of tap water. Drinking it is not an option, though I have found that a kettle of water boiled and left standing for a few hours becomes a great deal less offensive.

As I ride my bike home, one of my neighbours yells out to me: "If you think this is bad, wait until the boils get here." I laugh and smile and wave as I pass, but I am confused thinking of it as a water reference, and don't get the joke until I am almost home.

You see, day before yesterday a pair of tornadoes ripped through town, one heavily damaging the airport, and another running top to bottom through Lakeview, completely destroying the very few houses that had survived the flooding caused by the 17 th-Street canal breach. Then yesterday, with the wind and dropping water pressure, the fires started. Today there is no electricity, and the phones only receive, and we can't call out.

Boils and a plague of locusts cannot be far behind.

A person could get depressed.

They do. Our suicide rate is skyrocketing. During one single week in October, eight doctors, unknown to one another, took their own lives.

They could not stand the memory of what they had seen along with maintaining themselves in a malfunctioning and defective environment.

This place we call home on a daily basis.

Months have passed now, but the quality of life here has actually begun to slide downward again. A few weeks ago the United States president said he saw people here "with a spring in their step again." I wonder if he can have really left his airplane.

That said, my electricity just came on. I guess I will go shut down the generator, power up the computer and process these words.

Process these words about New Orleans.

They tell me I should be serious

A century and a half since New Orleans' first Mardi Gras and al-most six months since hurricane Katrina, the city's festive spirit defies Washington's neglect.

I have never used political correctness as an inhibitor of things I find amusing. Over my long years I have found much rough fodder for laugh-ter, and over these last long months I must admit crudity of subject matter has not once kept me from howling out loud.

But now, as a citizen of New Orleans, I am discouraged from smiling.

That is the word sent south this past week from the scions of our federal government in the hurricane-safe city of Washington DC. If we want dollars from the US Treasury to help us purchase our tickets out of reconstruction hell, we should exclude all thoughts of celebrating. Joyous abandon is out.

We should abandon Carnival.

Grim-faced bureaucrats, senators and representatives have paraded themselves in air-conditioned buses past our destroyed homes and busi-nesses for six months now, have stepped off their vehicles momentarily, and in front of pre-positioned microphones and lenses have declared us something-in-the-neighbourhood-of-a-disaster.

This qualification because some of the more fiscally-responsible law-makers who stood amidst the rubble of 400,000 damaged residential structures and 200,000 completely unsalvageable homes still hold reser-vations as to the severity of our loss.

To underline the stern conditions of our bail-out, they have declared that if we are going to get taxpayers' money, we should not be cele-brating.

This said on the cusp of the 150th anniversary of the first Mardi Gras parade.

The mystique and lure of Carnival bores deeply into the soul of the native New Orleanian. Jean Baptiste Le Moyne, Sieur de Bienville,

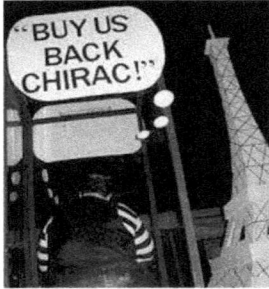

photo John d'Addario [1]

the founder and first governor of the Louisiana Territory, is said to have made his preliminary approach to the outskirts of what would become the city on Mardi Gras Day 1699, promptly naming the sluggish snake-infested creek that emerged from the nearby swamps as Bayou Mardi Gras. He then immediately headed for higher ground.

Bienville lacked a great party sensibility, but he at least understood the need for the acknowledgement of a necessary holiday.

Over three centuries later, on 11 February 2006 the Krewe de Vieux proclaimed "C'est Levee!" as its theme and rolled through Bywater, the Faubourg Marigny and the Vieux Carré neighborhoods with two thousand liquid-enhanced costumers marching amidst dozens of mule-drawn floats, all satirizing the humourless bureaucrats in control of their fates. One float entitled "Buy Us Back, Chirac!" once again reminded the world of our origins in a far less serious culture. I think we all agree these days, that even rule via Paris would be preferable to our current situation.

I laughed a great deal that night and did not feel guilty. I seldom feel guilt about happiness.

Of course I did not personally receive a cheque from FEMA.

Though you have to admire the attitude of some people who did. A friend of mine, a long-time bartender at Tujague's—which coincidentally was founded in 1856, the same year as the first Mardi Gras parade—recently took a portion of the proceeds of a FEMA payment for the complete destruction of her family home, and purchased C-cup breasts, which were attached to her body with much skill and taste. The new appendages accompanied her to Tujague's last week and were showcased for approval among us regulars. Quite a pleasant surprise, to look up from my bourbon and see such an exhibit. But again, I felt no guilt. In case any of you are coming to town, the new-found twins are expected to be on frequent display during the upcoming Carnival weekend.

Coincidentally, that is what Mardi Gras has come to be known for, the collegiate flesh and bead exchange on Bourbon Street. I suppose that's what the conservative politicians really think we are all doing down here this season. We should be out chopping away mould and raising sheetrock, scraping contaminated mud off our drives and flushing sewer lines, and instead we are debauching.

You know, after six months of the former, I am completely enamoured with the prospect of five days of the debauch option. With a moratorium on good taste.

The strip clubs on Bourbon Street, which have been flourishing with the numbers of relief workers, soldiers and carpetbaggers all these last months, are beginning to show a decline in patronage as the numbers of naked revellers on the streets increases. Why pay to be in a dark club, when there is this great free ongoing show outside?

I must admit that the inventiveness of those preferring nudity without incarceration has grown in recent years, especially as large numbers of talented airbrush artists have descended on the city. I have already made my first sighting, in the French Market yesterday. While unsuccessfully searching for fresh fruit—unsuccessfully because for the first time since 1791 there *is* no fresh produce in the market—I looked up and spied a young couple, male and female, shopping for beads. They were wearing socks and

Jim Gabour (right) with his brother

shoes. Though, due to the most amazing *trompe l'oeil* clothing that they had sprayed in a millimetre-thick layer of colour on their skins, I had to look twice, even thrice, to notice that they were truly naked.

"Mardi Gras Mambo, babies." All I could say.

Then I smiled.

This because I have once again taken a political/philosophical position for this carnival. We all do, those who mask religiously, in one way or another.

Simultaneously I am doing my bit to clean up the city as part of my carnival costuming.

I have been gathering lengths of the bright fluorescent "Caution" tape I have found littering the sites of demolished structures. As a further ironic indicator of the influx of migrant reconstruction workers, the tape is actually bilingual—it reads "Caution/Cuidado," the words printed in large black capital letters along its length.

Cuidado. I worry that irony may also not be allowed under the federal order. "Be serious," they have warned.

The logistics of a simple Mardi Gras costume: I am hot-gluing hundreds of feet of the Caution tape to an old raincoat, and converting a used orange rubber street-marker cone into a hat festooned with small orange gas-line marker flags. I have a small battery operated fan that I will carry in hand.

My theme: "Throw Caution to the Winds."

This attitude in place, I suspect my imminent arrest by the Gaiety Police may well be certain.

And come Tuesday eve, I may call upon you to furnish bail.

Mardi Gras Mambo, babies.

URLS

[1] www.flickr.com/photos/jonnodotcom/

Out of order

A Sunday afternoon bicycle-ride, and a jolt into the harsher realities of post-Katrina New Orleans.

I am eating aspirins and soaking in hot salt baths. I am recovering, not from the festivities of the New Orleans Mardi Gras but because, after six months, there has been no restoration of order in this city. Two-thirds of the traffic lights are non-functional, and those that do work are more often than not ignored by a populace now used to stopping perfunctorily, if at all, at corners and then roaring through.

And the carpetbaggers, our saviours, ignore traffic laws completely, knowing that the best the locals can do with their depleted traffic force is to stick a piece of paper on their car window and hope that, sooner or later, justice will somehow find the lawbreakers in Wyoming or Nebraska or New Mexico.

Or in my case, Florida.

I was returning home on my bicycle from a Sunday-afternoon "Nickle-a-Dance" live-music show at Café Brazil, four blocks from my house. I had seen the first half-hour of some 200 people dancing in the street to the twenty-piece New Oriental Leviathan Foxtrot Orchestra, an eclectic and lovable mix of musical oddballs who play obscure tunes from the first few decades of the 20th century.

I was elated—by the music, the great showing of locals and the weather, still perfect and sunny, with just enough heat for daytime comfort and just enough cool for night-time sleep. I had seen bees in my garden that day for the first time since Hurricane Katrina, and now had confidence that my wildly blooming avocado tree would be pollinated and furnish yet another crop of delectable fruit. I had finished my video editing for the day, with some progress, and was looking forward to reviewing the work when I returned home. My bicycle was humming along, dodging the potholes of Dauphine Street. I was content.

I approached the six lanes and wide central "neutral ground" (as we in New Orleans call the grassy expanse between opposing traffic lanes) of Elysian Fields Avenue, two blocks from home. The traffic lights at this major intersection had actually been repaired only a few days earlier, only to have a post-carnival driver ram the central light and again render them inoperable, though blinking red. In place of working lights stood nine stop signs, two to a traffic direction on the wide street and a single sign on one-way Dauphine. I came to the single sign, looked out onto the broad avenue and paused, balancing the bike.

Nothing immediately approaching. Pedestrian traffic all around, and a car behind me. I advanced. Third gear. Into the central lane. And then, out of the corner of my left eye, I saw the end of my life.

In the next lane, a small car was barrelling toward me, its owner jabbering into a mobile phone, his eyes unfocused on the centre of the road. Twenty feet away, he showed no sign of stopping, or even noticing the intersection, much less me. And I was pedalling directly into his path. I jerked on the rear brakes, but could tell instantly that there was not enough power there to keep me from the wheels of the car. I pulled the front brakes, and immediately flew over the handlebars, directly into the lane.

As my palms and knees hit the road surface, I could hear car tyres screaming, and just like in the movies, time spread before me. I could see the first day I drove back into town after the hurricane, coming off the Mississippi bridge ramp into downtown New Orleans to immediately be run to the side of the road by trucks coming backwards down a one-way street. I could see vehicles parked across all lanes of traffic on a major thoroughfare while their owners ate lunch on the hoods of their vehicles, heedless of the honks of the stalled traffic behind them. I could see the road rage of a man, asleep at the wheel with his engine running in the heart of the French Quarter, who, when I awoke him with a honk, ran to my window, glassy-eyed, and tried to jerk me from my car. I could see the hundreds, the thousands, of cars parked illegally by people who know that traffic-law enforcement is a low-priority item for the police and elected officials.

And now here, finally, looking at the black asphalt surface with some small degree of calm, I waited for the impact of a metal vehicle with my flesh.

It did not happen.

Pedestrians began screaming at the distracted driver: "Stop sign, you bum!" "Don't they teach you to drive where you came from?" "Somebody call the cops."

I stood up. A 20-ish tanned couple, both sandy blond, in a Nissan with Florida license plates, were looking about them like they had encountered a tribe of semi-humans who were after their valuable moveable goods and not-so-moveable heads. They rolled up their car windows and each, in one motion, raised a single finger and shook it at us.

These ridiculous, ungrateful people from New Orleans.

They drove on, laughing.

I picked up my bike. The very sweet lady in the pickup truck behind me got out to see if I was OK. A young gent with a pitch-black Mohawk and nose chains brought me my bicycle lock from where it had rolled in the middle of the street. I thanked them, and continued on my way.

Last night I dreamed myself back onto my bicycle, pedalling easily across level grassy plains toward a ridge on the far horizon. As I approached, though, a sense of dread overtook me, and I awoke.

I sat up.

"There's no order," I said aloud.

Thinking back now, in daylight, I believe that remains the storm's ultimate legacy.

The deliveryman's story

*"They up and forgot us, and that's when things got bad. Really
bad." Katrina comes knocking.*

He brought two chairs and a tale.

A week ago we reluctantly discarded two sofas and three rugs which,
even after repeated steam cleaning and saturation with deodorisers,
still carried The Smell. It stubbornly clung to the old fabric, even
the wood. Five weeks in a sealed house with a leaky refrigerator full
of rotting food and a neighbourhood surrounded by sewage and waste
ensured that nothing could remove or overwhelm the odour, or message,
or the mechanics, of death and decay.

So with no small amount of effort and the repeated use of a bent,
creaking dolly, we carried them out to the common mid-block trash
pile, and left them. The next morning they were all gone, on their way
to a new home, obviously appropriated by someone with a monstrous
head cold.

The odour diminished, then left, but the living-room was obviously
missing something essential, especially when we had one of the more-
and-more-infrequent post-hurricane guests. It was not as hospitable as
it had been before, with the comforting second-hand sofas and floor
coverings. In a burst of energy somehow linked with redefining ourselves and the city, we decided to buy something new. Not something
that, in our twenty-three year history of thrift stores and consignment
shops, we have often been able to do. Luckily I have kept working
throughout our displacement, and we had the wherewithal for a single
splurge.

So this weekend we went to H&M Inc, a century-old New Orleans firm
famous for overpriced but honest decorative furniture. The closest
store, a French Quarter outlet in an aged and appropriately welcoming
building, had lost its roof and most of its merchandise had been ruined,
so we drove out Airline Highway to the warehouse facility, a three-and-
a-half-storey behemoth which had only been flooded by two feet of
water on its bottom floor.

Amazing the building was open at all, but there it was, workmen still
painting and sheet-rocking, wiring and vacuuming.

The purchase itself was relatively painless and even entertaining. After
a solid half-hour of browsing and fabric ruffling, Faun eyed the chairs

she had selected as finalists. She squinted. She scanned the room, came to some sort of resolution, then walked over to a well-dressed woman and spoke persuasively to her. My partner is ingenious. She had espied a stranger who was wearing a blouse approximately the colour of our living room walls, and convinced her to be used in our search.

Faun asked the red-clad woman to sit in the chairs. She willingly did so. Faun squinted again and the woman watched as Faun held up a single finger, peered over its top, pointed to her left and made her decision. We'd take two of the rust-coloured chairs with the checks, she said. Two matching chairs.

My treat, I told her, a healing from the storm.

Since there is limited space in the VW bug convertible she drives, Faun asked that the rather massive chairs be delivered. The salesman—an amicable gent identified as Billy on his brass nametag—said they'd be at our door three days later. Billy was true to his word. And in that banal manner the deliveryman, the two chairs, and his story came into our home.

He was already on the front porch speaking with Faun when I came around from the back house. He was a head taller than me, a bit over six feet, with short hair, an engaging smile and a shirt embroidered with the H&M logo and his name: Andre.

I'd heard the loud diesel truck drive up, and come out to see the unloading of the new purchases. Andre had just introduced himself and remarked on how remarkably well our house had weathered the storm. Katrina is always the first conversational coin exchanged between locals these days. I inquired back with the appropriate response, asking how he had done.

"Not too bad," he said, with only the slightest hesitation. "Well, we lost our house, but we're all here and OK now. I got a picture here", he said as he pulled out a wallet and began searching the various pockets, "a picture of my wife and baby." He found the photograph, a rough trapezoidal fragment cut out of a larger Polaroid and then laminated with thick clear plastic. His wife looked young and content. "Alisha," said Andre. Alisha was wearing a shiny satin blouse and had a large well-shaped head of hair, glowing brown eyes, and a tiny smiling infant in her lap. A boy in a blue T-shirt, reaching for the photographer. "Andre Junior," Andre pointed. "There they are," he said, looking admiringly at the picture himself. "We came out together."

"Have a hard time?" I asked. "Well," he paused, a life mentor hesitating at the onset of teaching of an honest, necessary, and ultimately painful lesson. Then he told me.

"We stayed. My fault. Gotta say that first. We got a solid two-storey brick house out in Gentilly. Had it for six years and it never flooded before, never got the least bit of water since we been there. Plus I laid the new shingles myself, and the roof's solid, three-quarter-inch treated plywood underneath, so I figured we'd be fine. We was, until the levees broke, then the water started coming up so fast we had to scramble upstairs from the first floor before we could even get stuff out of it, the TV and all."

"That water came right behind us, waltzing up the stairs like it owned the place, and quick as a wink got to swirling around our ankles on the second floor, acting like we was nothing but unwanted visitors. Then the lights went out. Flash of light and popping of sparks when the transformer down the block blew. I was stacking stuff in the dark on the beds and chest of drawers, and hauling stuff to the attic best I could, thinking it would never stop."

"But the water finally topped out around my waist. Just stopped. I kept watch. It filled my pants pockets and then stopped like it had what it wanted."

"'Bout midnight, it was. I waded out on to the upstairs balcony from our bedroom to get a look. The water was running by my house just below the balcony railings and I could see this black oily surface going all around the block, filling streets and yards, with my neighbours' rooftops sticking through. For blocks and blocks. People was yelling, banging on the roofs of houses from the inside. They'd climbed up to get away from the water and got themselves stuck in their attics with no way to break out. Two days earlier the mayor had told everybody what was staying to make sure they had an axe in their house, especially in their attics. The news people, and the president even, had acted like the mayor was some sort of farm boy for saying such things."

"'Take your axes upstairs', he'd said, and those news folks had laughed. But here it was a-flooding, and that nasty water was drowning folks like rats in they own houses, and you better know them folks wished now that they had them axes."

"I couldn't tell where exactly the yelling was coming from, because everything was echoing off the water and spinning from every which way. But yessir, hollering and screaming was all around us. I went inside to make sure Alisha and Junior was OK. They wasn't, but I talked to 'em for a bit and they calmed down. We drunk some water out of the upstairs bathroom sink, figuring the water hadn't had time to get bad yet, but knowing we could be stuck here for a bit."

"'Twadn't that bad. Not that part. Because late the next morning a motorboat full of guys in uniform come along and got us out of there. I still don't know who they was, but got us out of our house and they took us to the Broad Street overpass, where there was maybe two-three hundred folks already waiting around. Nothing to do, no food, no water, no blankets, but I figured somebody would come directly. They wouldn't just leave us there, nossir."

"But they did, they left us. Then they up and forgot us, and that's when things started to get bad. Really bad."

"'Cause there was some no-account folks up there, and they were hassling the people who looked weaker and taking their money and food if they had any. They didn't bother us, at least for the first two nights, but I know they was looking to. Especially after that second night and into the third morning with no food, no water at all, more and more folks just wading and swimming up there and floating in on rafts and plastic swimming-pools and wheelbarrow tubs and all kinds of stuff. Folks were getting desperate and mean."

"Now all this time I been calling my sister uptown on my cell phone and it's going down and she's saying 'Get on up here right now. There ain't no flooding and I got running water and electricity and a working real phone.' But I've been looking down, and the water is deep at the end of the overpass. I know neither my wife nor baby can swim, and I ain't in the best of shape. So up to then we was sitting it out, just waiting and hoping and trying to stay invisible to The Bad Guys."

"Then about middle a the morning, it happened. Some baby, maybe eight years old, climbed up on the overpass railing, and as soon as he got to the top, he just slips and falls right over. Down maybe fifty feet and into the water. Everybody rush to that side and look for him, but he don't come up. And nobody goes down to try and get him, because even if you jumped off and didn't get killed, you'd have to swim a good half mile to the ramps to get back where you started. So we just saw that baby die and nobody did a thing. I could see the faces of the people that was stealing and robbing from folks. They saw that baby go down, and you could tell it didn't mean nothing to them. Not a thing."

"That's when I decided we had to go."

"I had seen this man down toward the end of things, toward the water on the west end of the overpass, sleeping on an air mattress. Lot of plastic tubes in a row, about three feet across, like one of those things you use to float in a swimming pool. I took the wife and baby and I went to him and I says, 'Look, man, I got to get my family out of here. I got to get to my sister's house uptown where it's safe for them, and I want to ask you to loan me that air mattress. Please', I says. And he looks me in the face and looks at the wife and child, and he gives me that mattress, not saying another word."

"So we go down to the water and I get Alisha and Andre Jr on that mattress and I start pushing and wading. It don't take fifty feet before I am up to my neck and they both are crying and wanting to go back. But I keep on, not wanting to see no more of that overpass."

"We making good time until maybe three hours later, about halfway uptown, I feel the mattress bump into something big floating in the water. I tell Alisha to move it out the way, and she holds out her hand and pushes and it turns over and it's a dead man, mouth open, face all puffed up something bad, and he bobs on up to the mat. She starts screaming and pointing and she falls off the mat into the water right by this dead guy. I quick get around to the side to hold Junior on, and push that dead man away. And then I grab Alisha and holler at her to stop and try and get her up on the mat again so we can get going. For a bit there I think I am gonna have to tie her up with my belt to get her calmed down and lying quiet on the mattress, but finally she gets better and we make it to my sister's place."

"About a week later we all got evacuated to Charlotte, North Carolina, and I got no complaints about that. Folks was nice to us, took care of us and made sure we was OK. They went out of their way to make us feel like we was worth something. I figure I owe 'em for that."

"So ever since I been back and on the delivery truck again, I go out of my way to find somebody what needs something, every day. And I try to help, help somebody every day. Makes me feel good."

"So where did you want these chairs, ma'am?"

Election daze

The citizens of New Orleans are voting for a new mayor and for assessors who will calculate their property values and taxes. A wary eye on the city's post-Katrina politics.

The small envelope, dated mid-September 2005, arrived at my New Orleans mailbox on the morning of 12 April 2006. Seven months after it was mailed. The city's elections, only half as tardy, will arrive tomorrow, 22 April. I have examined both, and have found, once again, that every detail of post-K life carries a connecting theme.

The deadline for the event described in the September mail was November 2005. I lost that opportunity. The belated election? By the fluke of an unexpected piece of out-of-town work, I am now stranded in Los Angeles, scheduled on election-day to fly from southern California to Las Vegas for a second four-day shoot, without a chance of diverting home Saturday to cast my vote.

I am not sure this is a bad thing. The situation at least lets me allow myself the excuse of absence, when in fact both my partner and I have been torn for weeks on a mayoral choice [1], the most important of the elections. Before I left for the airport, we discussed the matter again over coffee, as she would now be casting the house's sole vote.

Impasse. Neither of us had/has the slightest idea of who should get our endorsement, even after all this concerned soul-searching.

We both feel manipulated and left without a real choice in an electoral process that will determine what physically, economically, and emotionally happens to us in the immediate and far-reaching future.

Of course, in spite of Katrina, this is not the first time such a situation has arisen in a place many describe as "the northernmost city in the Caribbean."

I remember hearing my truthful-to-a-fault college roommate, who remains my best friend after decades, assess Louisiana political situations upon almost every election. He would size up the candidates, taking his time over a matter of weeks if not months. He would read other individual's and organisation's assessments of the candidates. He studied. He was careful. Analytical. He actually cared about government, while I was somehow still marooned in fantasising over the possibility of a less-than-democratic voting-booth encounter with some willing female independent.

I was not astute in such high-flying matters, and would wait for Al's judgment.

Inevitably, he presented a candid and accurate analysis.

But it seemed that each time, after all that work, he would end up giving the same speech when it came to summarising a Louisiana election.

Even after our long separation, I remember his inevitable pronouncements, something very close to this: "Jimbo, I have done my homework. You know that to be true. I have examined the personal traits and public backgrounds of every candidate. I have looked at previous offices held, and votes cast for and against vital issues."

"Even disregarding recurring past situations, I have reached the only possible conclusion: that we are, at this very moment in history, once again shit out of luck."

Colourfully spoken, he was politically correct, in its truest sense. Every time.

I fear that his analysis holds true today. Undermining a deep desire to make a difference with my vote.

On the eve

Tomorrow will be election-day [2] in New Orleans, even as I pack cameras to film an early morning sparring match between a Grammy-award-winning trumpeter and an ex-heavyweight boxing champion.

I have given the situation back home further consideration, and have decided that there actually is one race in April 2006, and only one, in which I hold high interest. I had forgotten, amidst all the clamour over the mayor's race. There is another post [3] to be elected, a public figure who might truly affect the vagaries of New Orleans government, and I am damnably sorry that by my absence I will not have a say in its outcome. The city will vote for a public figure who is currently running in seven separate races, but whom the majority of New Orleans voters hope becomes only one at race's end.

Assessor. That is the job title—except in New Orleans's antiquated and bloated system of government, the city is broken into seven tax districts, each with its own assessor applying pressure on his constituents to continually re-elect him or her by threatening the instant doubling or trebling of the homeowner's property values, and thus the taxes owed.

Over the many, many years this system has been in place, countless occurrences of uneven, illegal and/or immoral use of the office have been documented, and polls for the last twenty years have shown that the population of the city wants one single fair-handed assessor. But the assessors themselves have always wielded enough power to keep legislators in check and any reforms at arm's length. They did so again in both legislative sessions since the storm, despite the overwhelming outrage at public officials acting completely contrary to public opinion.

But Katrina gave the assessors even more power [4] in this election. In the wake of the storm, every house in town is being reassessed, damaged or no—my own house included, though it received no appreciable damage at all—and all homeowners have received innocuous letters from their assessors, stating that the assessment is ongoing, but that they (the individual assessors) are on our side; i.e., they will adjust our assessments personally to make sure all is done properly.

These letters were all mailed and received the week before the election. The not-so-veiled threat here is: "Vote for me, or before I leave office I will send you a tax bill which you will never forget."

I remember my roommate's conundrum.

Ah yes, Al, but this time we may not be completely "shit out of luck."

Into the foray come seven individuals, non-politicians who are working in concert with much active backing from the population, one running against each of the current assessors. They are running as the "IQ" ticket. "IQ" = "I Quit," which is what each has promised to do if elected. The seven newcomers have proposed that they be elected to then hire an independent professional company to take over the duties of the assessor's office, and as soon as that company is in place, all seven will as one resign and leave tax assessments to professionals. There will be government oversight, but basically taxes will then be administered on a level playing field and there will be seven less corrupt, malingering bureaucrats to leech the tax dollars of the citizens of New Orleans.

Politicians who want you to vote them out of office. Now that is a vote I wish I could have cast.

URLS

[1] edition.cnn.com/2006/POLITICS/04/21/new.orleans.elex/
[2] www.nola.com/elections/
[3] seattlepi.nwsource.com/national/1135AP_New_Orleans_Election_QA.html
[4] www.nola.com/frontpage/t-p/index.ssf?/base/news-5/1144994419105110.xml

The choice is not choice

"The election is upon me and I have no idea which lever I will pull." The quandary of post-Katrina politics in New Orleans.

The language of the southern United States is one of polite obfuscation. It is often hard to get to the point of a conversation with all the personal inquiries, compliments and un-modern courtesy cluttering things up. So many words are spoken, all designed to merely make the other person feel comfortable, that many times in my life I have walked away from a New Orleans street-corner encounter feeling good, but wondering what was actually said.

Southern politeness can be a hazard in everyday life. I am a southern boy [1], born and bred, as they say. I was trained to show respect for ladies and my elders, take my hat off indoors, put my hand over my mouth when I sneeze, never use profanity in front of clergy, and to always offer other people considerations first.

Therefore one fine afternoon up north in New York City, at 22 years of age I was more than taken aback when I met my first modern woman, a person who literally screamed at me for five long minutes in front of a large, interested but embarrassed crowd of strangers. My crime: opening a door and offering a courteous nod of the head to allow a lady to pass through first. *La Moderne* was insulted mightily at my actions, and she let me know that in graphic, anatomically-referenced terms.

This does not happen in New Orleans.

As a somewhat convoluted but universally-applicable example of this need for politeness, I offer an old chestnut, about the disdain for certain activities among southern belles. It still rings true in 2006:

Q: Why do southern women never have group sex?

A: They can't spare the time to send out that many "thank you" notes.

Decorum and decision

And so to the 2006 mayor's race [2].

Twenty-five candidates initially [3] filed official paperwork to run for the office, as the current mayor seemed such an easy mark that anyone could unseat him, but by the time the real political machinery began this number had dwindled to just over a dozen. Of those there remained a few outrageous entries, some funny, some frightening.

But after all the hubbub of the primaries, there remain only two [4], Mitch Landrieu and the incumbent, Ray Nagin. And they are polite to a fault, knowing that whoever loses in the run-off vote on 20 May, he will have to work with the winner the very day after the election. To keep the city afloat, and undivided.

"Undivided," because many pundits say the vote will come down to race [5], that blacks will be loyal to Nagin and whites to Landrieu in a city now almost evenly divided in that regard.

This generalisation may be the opposite of reality. Many whites feel Landrieu is too liberal. And, because US senator Mary Landrieu [6] is such an opponent of the president, they feel strongly that Mitch in office is a detriment to getting federal aid. At the same time a large portion of the "chocolate city" contingent feel that Nagin is already too much of a loose cannon (and mouth), and that he has lost the credibility to be able ever again to rally the national cooperation necessary for the city's rebuilding.

They are an interesting pair.

As I said, both are polite.

Mitch Landrieu [7], the state's lieutenant-governor, is the son of former mayor Moon Landrieu, and the brother of aforementioned Mary Landrieu. There are judges and appointees by the score, all bearing the same surname. The family is a stream of politicians that runs through New Orleans like mud down the Mississippi. And any farmer will tell you that alluvium may be sloppy and occasionally inconvenient, but it also guarantees the fertility of the river's delta.

I cannot fault the family [8] on large issues. They are good people, by and large, and seem well-intentioned.

But there are questions about both Mitch's future ambitions—will he be running for governor very shortly? And his focus—is he already looking beyond the city?

The Landrieus have always done well with the African-American community. Mitch's dad broke all precedents for racial inclusion during his tenure as mayor. Everyone loved Moon Landrieu. And as a Catholic, he also crossed over to appeal to the French Creole community, in spite of liberal attitudes toward abortion, divorce, and the separation of church and state.

Mitch Landrieu's base of support transcends race, he will tell you.

I have known the current mayor, Ray Nagin [9], personally, since we both worked at a local television cable company some years back. He was occupied first as an accountant and then general manager. I was executive producer in programming. He is a gentleman, one of the most likable men I have ever met, sensible and honest. I voted for him the first time he ran for office.

He is slightly more centrist than Landrieu, also is Catholic, and appeals to many of the city's more conservative pastors, both white and black.

But there are questions being weighed about Ray's continued capability to govern effectively after the many recent, high-profile gaffes. I have heard the argument that, post-Katrina, he should be awarded a two-year vacation, and then we should let him come back and be mayor again without an election, out of gratitude for getting us this far. I am not sure that even Ray would object to that at this point.

Another friend suggested that a re-elected Nagin [10] would be good for the city, because if elected this time he would then face term-limits—no re-election—and would not be afraid to make the hard choices that we all know are now necessary.

I wonder.

For his first term, the white community voted overwhelmingly for Nagin the non-politician, Nagin the businessman, and there once lay his strength.

Things are different in a post-Katrina world [11]. The candidates have been meeting in debates every night these last two weeks, and have developed a forced cordiality onstage that somehow reminds me of that "southern belle" story.

I have no idea if voting for the least-polite of the candidates might actually be voting for the most-forceful. The election is upon me and I have no idea which lever I will pull.

All I know is that I will awake this Sunday morning, walk out front to pick up the newspaper, and with the depleted but valiant population of New Orleans, look at a headline to discover our mutual fates.

Wish us luck, world. We'll be sure to send "thank you" notes.

URLS

[1] www.jimgabour.com

[2] www.nola.com/elections/
[3] www.opendemocracy.net/articles/article_3469.jsp
[4] msnbc.msn.com/id/12821264/
[5] www.csmonitor.com/2006/0519/p03s03-uspo.html
[6] landrieu.senate.gov/hurricanes/index.cfm
[7] www.crt.state.la.us/ltgovernor/biography.aspx
[8] www.msnbc.msn.com/id/9558118/site/newsweek/from/RL.1/
[9] www.cityofno.com/Portals/Portal35/portal.aspx
[10] www.iht.com/articles/2006/05/18/news/nagin.php
[11] news.bbc.co.uk/1/hi/world/americas/4628000.stm

Frozen assets: letter from New Orleans

A broken, fearful city faces the start of the hurricane season looking for a saving grace.

Modern American political history is defined by petty criminals.

My mother and I normally find ourselves on the same side of political debates, but we love each other enough to completely avoid any discussion of our religious differences. That is why she quickly gained my attention when she called this morning from the house on Bayou Robert to announce that she is now attending Mass daily. Here in New Orleans at the other end of the line, I rolled my eyes, figuring the time had probably come again for another of those much-dreaded, once-a-decade pushes at Saving Jim's Soul [1].

But she had something else on her mind.

"It's Bush I have to thank," she told me.

This got my attention.

"I told Father Ryan that after Mass just today," she went on, "but he looked at me funny, because he knows your father and I are yellow-dog Democrats." (By way of explanation, *Yellow Dog* in the deep south identifies a dyed-in-the-wool Democrat, indicating that such a person would vote for a yellow dog if he ran under the party banner.)

Another dramatic pause ensues as she let this formidable collision of religion and politics settle into my consciousness.

"But Father Ryan would have been even more upset if he knew what I was praying for at church these last weeks."

Pause and a breath.

"Okayyyy..." I said. I knew she wanted to be led down the road to whatever it was she was going to say. It was my duty to give the appropriate prompts.

"Well, after all that has been going on in Washington, and the terrible things that have been happening here and elsewhere because of our government, I have been praying steadfastly for one thing. I know it's wrong and I know it is not logistically or even legally possible, but I have been praying for it."

She paused again, and I could feel her looking at the phone, willing me to do my part.

I did. "Annndddd..."

"I have been praying that God would somehow bring back the adulterer."

A city adrift

Mom always admired the fact that Clinton's sins harmed no one but himself. She feels that this is the highest level of politician that we can realistically hope for in this country.

History does nothing but reinforce her belief, from the legend of our initial president George Washington cutting down a tree—though admitting his "crime"—to Richard M Nixon's trifling burglary, an act that brought an end to a tortured and corrupt tenure, another decade that saw American lives reduced to fodder for governmental power squabbles.

Now comes this fellow from New Orleans, US Representative William Jefferson [2], a long-time office-holder who for years has pushed the envelope on inserting his family onto governmental payrolls. His sister Betty is one of the city's much-derided assessors, and herself has been the subject of numerous investigations concerning the use of her office for personal gain.

Jefferson's daughter Jamila, with the ink on her law diploma barely dry, immediately ran for public office though she had no experience whatsoever in government, other than as an aide watching her father's machinations. She failed in that election, despite an enormous influx of campaign cash from dad's cronies, but with even more money she won in a second try at state representative.

Jamila then immediately allowed her father to hire her as the lawyer to organise the shell company through which he would funnel his bribe money. For that, she received [3] tens of thousands of dollars in fees, much more than her annual official salary. She was still hanging in the wings waiting for the next political spoil when the Feds revealed their investigation.

Representative Jefferson [4] may not now be able to support her next attempt.

Although the search of his Capitol office by the justice department is said to have precipitated a "constitutional crisis," and in spite of the intervention of the president to seal all the confiscated material, the overwhelming quantity and quality of evidence against the man would seem to lead his constituents to doubt his veracity.

Caught red-handed, as was our first president, he will not admit to the cutting of the Washingtonian cherry-tree.

This may be due to lack of imagination as much as personal avarice.

His homes, and those of his cohorts [5], have now been raided by the justice department on numerous occasions. One of the first legal intrusions turned up $10,000 in packets of $100 bills, neatly wrapped and concealed inside a food freezer: an amusing but hardly original method of safeguarding one's totally-legal family fortune. Now, months later, we are told that up in Washington DC another freezer was discovered to hold $90,000, the same amount of money that was earlier handed over to Jefferson by an informant in front of FBI cameras and recorders. Except that now the bills were suitably chilled and preserved for future long-term spending.

There is more to this story [6], but the backdrop makes the substantial legal case seem trivial.

The backdrop is New Orleans, now a few thousand homes clustered along the banks of The Mississippi River, a human settlement totally at the mercy of an already-dysfunctional government and a failed [7] infrastructure. A place where the pipes and lines that feed the city are cracked and bleeding, worsening an already bad situation. Forty percent of the city is still without hope of electricity and when a neighborhood is finally turned on, fires erupt at random. The sewerage-and-water board now pumps three million gallons of water daily to get one million gallons into the homes of residents; which means that every day, two million gallons leak out to further erode the already tenuous soil base which supports the city. Only 2,000 of 22,000 pre-Katrina [8] businesses have returned.

And in a few days a new hurricane season [9] will be upon us. We are at a critical point in our history and our lives.

William Jefferson represents this city in Washington. He is no longer concerned with his constituents' plight as much as his own, even while (Republican) George W Bush protects (Democrat) William Jefferson's rights to suppress evidence of wrongdoing.

Barring prosecution for his own assault on the constitution, Bush is guaranteed almost three more years in office.

Jefferson may have considerably less time in public service, especially if additional caches of frozen assets are discovered.

My mother continues to pray.

For the return of the adulterer.

URLS

[1] www.jimgabour.com
[2] www.house.gov/jefferson/biography.shtml
[3] www.bayoubuzz.com/articles.aspx?aid=7275
[4] www.npr.org/templates/story/story.php?storyId=5448308
[5] www.washingtonpost.com/wp-dyn/content/article/2006/06/04/AR2006060400816.html
[6] www.editorandpublisher.com/eandp/news/article_display.jsp?vnu_content_id=1002613013
[7] www.opendemocracy.net/articles/article_2811.jsp
[8] www.opendemocracy.net/articles/article_2801.jsp
[9] www.nola.com/hurricane/

Urban renewal

Post-Katrina New Orleans has become a city of firearms, fears and feral gangs. Welcome to life under siege.

My neighbourhood was surrounded today.

By the same Humvees, troops and large-calibre machine guns that surround villages in Iraq and Afghanistan.

Roadblocks were put in position across streets, and men in camouflage helmets and bullet-proof vests have started searching house-to-house.

The worst part is, I welcome it.

For the last months, increasingly large gangs of feral animals from across America have begun to congregate here, knowing how easy it is to hide among mile after mile of crushed, abandoned, open homes. The word is out that the New Orleans police department is in disarray.

The word is correct.

Gangs have the upper hand, and two days ago five teenagers, cruising a neighbourhood at four in the morning, were all gunned down by multiple automatic weapons, in what was just a minor salvo in exponentially developing turf wars. Homes and possessions are being fought over by groups of humans who wish to prey on those of us foolish enough to love, and refuse to leave, this godforsaken place.

And personally, I must say that I would prefer they kill each other, rather than kill me.

The gunfire that had been stilled by Katrina has now come back at night, repeated staccato rhythms that before the storm had become so frequent here that I could, and still can, identify the weapons.

I would hear a shallow popping, six to eight quick bursts in rapid succession, and read in the morning paper that two individuals had been gunned down nearby with a Glock 9.

So that's a Glock 9.

I awaken well before dawn, brought out of my dreams by a deep thudding, a *whup-whup* sound that seems to go on forever. Then it stops briefly, allows a few breaths' worth of echo, and resumes, to finish with ten more seconds of diminishing resonance. Over coffee, TV's morning news tells me an AK-47 was used to riddle a drug-dealer and his luxury sedan. A fingerprint-less weapon was recovered at the murder scene, an AK-47 supplemented by an empty double-banana clip, enabling it to piggy back two twenty-shot magazines.

So that's an AK 47.

Now, just now, as the mailman delivers the daily packet of whatever struggling mail gets through, I see three national guardsmen, each armed with an M-16 automatic weapon, cruise by the front of my house in an armoured vehicle.

I wave. They wave back.

I know what an M-16 sounds like, too. And I know what it can do to human flesh.

The rest of the world thinks the crisis in New Orleans is over and that things are getting back to normal. Or, they are sick of hearing stories about what they perceive as a city inhabited by whiners. I guess I am one of those whiners.

But allow me:

Our water is completely cut off every other day. Hot water tanks empty and shudder and boiling fluid spits from open faucets until lines fill again. The rest of the time water pressure is so low that fire hydrants are all but non-functional. Helicopters with bags are now the main source of fire dousing.

Eighty-five million gallons—the city confirmed the official figure on 19 June—of water are now lost *every day* through cracked pipes, seeping into the soil. The city is below sea level already, with the water table right at the soil top, so this much additional flow is causing many of the remaining undamaged houses to sink and topple from their foundations and piers.

What water does get through to homes is undrinkable, doctored with so much chlorine to rid it of bacteria that a glass of water is almost literally a glass of bleach.

Bottled-water services are understaffed and overwhelmed by demand for drinkable water, so numerous occasionally dangerous home remedies have been concocted to make tap water palatable.

Electricity is available to only 40% of the city. I am lucky and have access to power at my own home. But even here the juice pops out three-four times a day, causing multiple fires when it surges back on. An incredible commercial museum of irreplaceable Mexican "day of the dead" artifacts, six blocks away, caught fire in just such a surge night before last.

My house, like most others in this neighbourhood, is full of blinking electric clocks. New Orleanians have given up on resetting indicators of time. We know that any reference to the present will just go away again in a few minutes.

Funny, but that's the way most of us have come to think of the whole experience of living here. Just ignore the fact that progress has gone away, again and again. And again.

No sense knowing what time it is, is it? Not in New Orleans, in any case.

More stoplights have come back, but between lost relief-workers crashing into them, and frequent gangster car chases, at least a quarter of the lights have been re-damaged and still do not work. Half the missing street-signs, one-way signs and stop signs in the city have not been replaced.

An especially frightening phenomenon: the gangs have been switching one-way signs' directions to confuse both the cops and nearby residents, to keep people out of neighbourhoods where they are marshalling their forces and hiding their loot. There is, if you obey the signs, no way to get into certain blocks of empty houses. And there the Bad Guys congregate, invisible.

They use stolen trucks and SUVs for their commerce, and they prowl rebuilding neighbourhoods at night, looting the same houses three and four times.

They wait for locals to install new appliances or piping, or doors and windows, in their gutted houses. And then, when the residents go back to their temporary homes at night, the looters run free, taking whatever they find.

In the morning the rebuilders return, of course, to find that, once again, they have lost everything.

One neighbourhood away, in broad view on an empty lot, the looters sell what they stole the night before at bargain basement prices, telling potential buyers that, by having low prices, they are doing their part to "help rebuild New Orleans." I have heard several stories of people who bought such material being followed home discreetly by the sellers, only to discover the next day that the same material had been stolen again, on the day it was purchased. Then the looters move to yet another neighbourhood, buying and selling the same material many times before again moving on.

Killing each other to remain dominant as the sole supplier in a certain part of town.

Using Uzis to assert their right to sell drugs and doorways.

That is why, the government tells me via the media, that after nine months going on ten, I personally am again under a rough form of martial law.

I want to complain. I want to say that it is not right.

But I live in New Orleans.

And I am a whiner, you see.

Kick out the jambs

In a sweltering, sinking New Orleans, there are signs of life reviving.

Yes, the heat in New Orleans is life-stifling, and we've still over two months of it to weather, along with the possibility of other meteorological intrusion.

Walking into the central business district to do errands, I find myself sprinting between shadows to avoid prolonged exposure to the sun. Before I park my car, I plot routes to my destination through the hallways of interconnected, air-conditioned buildings.

After 2005's surfeit [1] of water, we find ourselves in a drought of historic proportions: the deepest since records have been kept. Though we actually do not need the rain for irrigation, we look for something, anything to make a dent in the heat. Precipitation finally came and went yesterday, providing some small amount of relief. Even though drain systems showed by their performance—many low intersections were flooded—that the city's pumps are not yet quite ready for another Big One.

Meanwhile, underground, the literal rivers escaping the city's water mains continues unabated. Plants are literally exploding into growth, as the poisonous filth from flooding is purged along with native soil. And while residences and businesses complain of chronic low water-pressure, the cracks in the public system guarantee that flora will be constantly watered.

The plants are grateful. Bursts of colour from flowers, lush ferns and palms frame piles of debris and the few remaining abandoned cars.

I spent the past weekend drilling new holes in the door jambs. There's a fun task, and more than a bit frightening when you consider that the house is settling so rapidly with the city's water line leaks that the deadbolts and doors wouldn't lock. And an unsecured home is not something you care to have in this town. Not these days. Maybe not ever.

In measuring and re-boring the jambs, I discover that my house has dropped a full 0.375 of an inch (9.5 millimetres) in the last ten months.

So, there's life: the water is higher and New Orleans lower. And hotter.

The gnostic jambs

Yesterday I sent the above paragraphs to my long-time best-friend Al, a gent whom I have mentioned in these columns before. He responded, first discussing the wily transgressions of a vagrant raccoon on his house in Austin, Texas—it has learned how to operate his electrical breaker-switches, and had turned off his air-conditioning.

Then he appraised the current siege of New Orleans. Like the 'coon, Al is a joker, and again, a learned one. He set the next three paragraphs on the e-table:

"If you look into Gnosticism, you'll find that the Gnostics believe there is an inverted version of the Sephiroth (the "tree of life"). This universe of unreality that reflects the real universe is, they believe, the so-called "astral plane."

The two meet—or at least, touch—at the boundary between the two versions of Malkuth, at "the veil," the sort of borderland between waking and sleeping consciousness, between the conscious and the Jungian unconscious. And unreality can leak into material manifestation at this interface. The lower the level of spirituality in a person or group of people, the more likely this leakage is. Of course, such leakage is most likely in large cities, NY, LA, NO...

And so there you go. A simple and post-scientific explanation for this mess warming: "Hell itself is leaking into this here world."

Yeah, Al, along with everything else, I think we must indeed have got ourselves some serious Hell leakage in this very neighbourhood.

From my own very-real sense of unreality, I would speculate there must even be a "veil" of sorts nearby. I would also think it easily used by creatures with a passport to unreality more valid than that which I possess. Like my own pre-Katrina [2] raccoon—yes, I had one, too—who hasn't come back to the house, though I think he's living in the abandoned fire station that adjoins the back of our property. In the days before the storm, he didn't do much that affected my everyday existence, except for leaving very artful arrangements of tracks on the outside table, eating my favourite fish out of the water garden, and crapping on the roof outside the second-floor bedroom's windows.

But he's not returned. Maybe it's because I've lowered all the upstairs blinds to keep the heat out and AC in—the short and furry voyeur got bored with nothing to watch, and no kitties to taunt.

So no 'coon, but just yesterday one pair of mating green parrots finally returned to the solitary remaining tree here at 725 Marigny, squawking and making a helluva racket. There were a dozen or more living here late last summer, a colourful and lively colony that gave me huge amounts of pleasure, but now just the two have come back to nest. I am quite glad to see any of them at all, and am taking an inordinate amount of comfort at the raucous sounds and small limbs that come crashing down from the crown of the ragged hackberry tree.

I think these unregulatable and self-confident birds may prove you correct, and that maybe they did indeed take refuge on the "other side" for the storm. They are, after all, themselves rather unreal in colour, shape and sound—and they have now decided that New Orleans is slightly better than Hell, and have returned.

After your letter, I think that I, too, am possibly slipping back and forth and just don't notice the difference.

URLS

[1] news.bbc.co.uk/1/hi/in_depth/americas/2005/hurricane_katrina/default.stm
[2] earthobservatory.nasa.gov/NaturalHazards/shownh.php3?img_id=13089

All done with mirrors

New Orleans is a permanent lesson in the shaping of personal identity.

Categorising, creating order, makes humans feel safer.

With all the newcomers in town, I constantly overhear people defining both me and my home town. "Creole" is one of the two identifying tags that are constantly and inappropriately placed on things New Orleans. The other is "Cajun". But more on that rampant misdescription later.

Tujague's restaurant, a personal favourite, can document it's Creole lineage. 151 years ago Guillame Tujague and his neighbor Madame Begue, who ran the breakfast shop next door and eventually joined forces with the larger restaurant, practically defined the genre as far as food goes. Only Antoine's restaurant is older, and again like most of the grande dame eating establishments of this town, still has descendants of the original owners working the floor daily.

The term "Creole" does hold some long and deep roots in New Orleans, its culture, and its food. It has, however, undergone many transformations. In the eighteenth century, the first settlers within the walls of the city, then mostly white, called themselves Creoles, a general term by which they labeled native residents. The word was then already being used in much the same manner by the *gens de couleurs*, the "free men of colour" in the West Indies.

The famous French writer Alexandre Dumas was himself descended from such stock on the island of Haiti. His father was a distinguished general in the service of Napoleon at around the same time boatloads of Africans were being brought to America in chains. Besides fighting, the elder Dumas had a reputation as a ladies' man of the first order. His son was a chip off the old *chaise lounge*.

After a life of numerous contributions to world literature, along with the action-filled adventures of *The Three Musketeers* and other voluminous works, Alexandre, who himself held considerable appetites both at table and in bed, spent many of the last years of his life sequestered in the countryside writing a 1,500-page cookbook with his lovely female chef. The young woman finally despaired both of her employer's culinary intentions, and the unrepressed desires of the local "bumpkins", and returned to Paris. Dumas was not far behind. He also hungered for the variety of the city, both culinary and feminine. Even earlier in his life, he had boasted of the company of "thousands" of women.

When he died, the unhealthily corpulent writer was once again en-
snared in the grips of a notorious love affair with a woman fifty years
his junior. Dumas was both enamored of, and infamously used by, Adah
Mencken, a famous Parisian dancer who was known—appropriately—
throughout Paris by the name "The Naked Lady". Adah cajoled
Alexandre into posing for photos with her, then without his permission released them to the press to enhance her own image as the most
sought-after woman in Paris. Dumas finally retired from the city in
frustration and humiliation.

I mention this only because Adah Mencken was, coincidentally, a native
of New Orleans.

"Creole" here in the city, in terms of humanity, came to be defined as
"of mixed heritage", partially a result of the Quadroon and Octoroon
balls of the 19th century at which free young women of colour were
exhibited by their mothers as prospects to become the mistresses of
wealthy white plantation owners. And thus gain property and separate
income for the family in perpetuity. Many fortunes were established
on the firm but resilient loins of these ingénues.

An indicator of the aesthetics of the day was the test for admission
to these economically advantageous affairs: as they approached the
door to the ballroom, a paper bag was held next to the faces of the
aspiring young women. If their skin tone was lighter in hue than the
bag, then they could "pass" for white and were allowed entry. And
thus, based on the ingredients available to the local paper mills, were
entire generations courted and born.

A Creole in New Orleans has a dash of many distinguished flavors:
English, African, Caribbean, Spanish, French, native American, ad-
venturer, philanderer.

And the Creole cooking for which New Orleans is deservedly famous
holds the same variety of spice and ingredient.

All this definition said and noted, I must reaffirm the opposite: it is
desperately hard to impose a strict category on anything in this town.

Insecticide

The neighbourhood corner where the Cuban grocery once stood is now a site for looters and dealers to sell their wares. It's a microcosm of New Orleans's wider battle.

You might not have ever even known your home was infested.

Then, one early morning you find yourself stumbling home after a long night of music, leaving the parade sounds of the Frenchmen Street club scene and entering the much quieter residential portion of the Faubourg Marigny.

After five hours of clubbing, yours is a slow walk, a step-by-step pace, mind pushing body through a seemingly endless wall of steaming, cloying fog. Your clothes drip with a combination of swirling airborne moisture and the sweat generated by your passage home. At this time of year, New Orleans maintains the summer's heat throughout the night, and movement takes great effort.

At 3am the fog seems alive, resisting your passage. She is a physical creature set internally aglow by the few unbroken streetlamps, her eerie flesh wrapped about a softly diffused skeletal structure, the blackened bones of stark, storm-ravaged Washington Square oaks. Their shadowed limbs embrace sidewalks and wrought-iron fences with thin fingers moving ever so slightly in a rare breeze.

And there is motion beyond that, all but concealed in the fog. *Something there.*

A bit of a shiver travels up the spine. You are reminded once again that *this is a dangerous place.* In the short term, close attention to the walking process is a necessity, despite the residual demands of the evening's beverages, and the continued echoing of a horn section in your ears.

An instant later you awaken, a zombie magically transported the last few blocks without incident—"I don't *remember* crossing Elysian Fields Avenue..."—standing at your front door, key in lock, still sweating profusely.

And suddenly you are desperate for a glass of cold water.

There follows a quick transit of living room and dining room to the kitchen. You reach out in the darkness, fumbling on the wall beside the door, until you find what you are looking for and flick on the lights.

You are blinded for a moment and then look down to see the counter-tops alive and moving.

"My god! What is *this*?" you yell over-loudly at the receding hordes. The cat awakens and runs into the kitchen knocking over a pot, yowling, knowing someone, or something, must be at his tuna.

Roaches. Omnipresent elsewhere since Katrina. But *not in this house*. Without thinking, you blindly smash dozens of insects with your hands.

Weeks later, even after the fumigation is complete and the insects gone, the memory still makes your skin crawl.

Who owns the 'hood'?

In the last two weeks, the National Guard has become the switched-on 200-watt light bulb in New Orleans' night, and the vermin are scurrying for safety. Oddly enough, the drug-dealers and looters seem emboldened at being flushed, and small groups are somehow reappearing in every neighbourhood, many brazenly doing their business in the open. In daylight.

Like on my very street-corner.

Yesterday I opened the front door, hedge-trimmers in hand, to find three New Orleans police department (NOPD) cars, half a dozen police officers and a Humvee full of soldiers, all milling about, going in and out of properties at the intersection two houses up the street. They looked very serious and several had their weapons in their hands.

And again, I was glad to see them. That corner, inhabited before The Storm by the *El Palaceno* Cuban Grocery, had been a neighbourhood centre for decades, serving steamed yucca, four kinds of fresh bananas and plantains, Cuban roast pork and pastries, and double-sized home-made tamales in corn shucks. It had been robbed before, but the Castro family refused to desert the community. People gathered on the kerbs to eat rich food off plastic plates and converse about work and home life.

But to the grocery, the looting after Katrina was complete and vile in its extreme. The family abandoned New Orleans, and the extended community of *El Palaceno* will never return. There was a vacuum, an *unfulfilment* of sorts left on this once-powerful corner, and the dealers, chased out of other parts of the city, were drawn to it.

For the last few weeks they have been showing up late at night to pursue their drive-by business, and just recently began staying on, often through whole days, drinking and dealing and harassing locals.

My neighbour, a large and intimidating street musician, had enough of it a few days ago and not only started calling the situation in to the cops, but walking right up to the dealers and yelling in their faces until they began to back off the corner and look for escape. He has a great bass blues voice and knows how to throw it to the back of a large crowd without amplification. The dealers heard him, took note and temporarily disappeared.

The two women at the other end of the block picked up the challenge and began harassing dealers from their balcony, too, calling in the NOPD every time they saw a dealer approach the street. And now the guard, noticing the shift from the dead areas back into surviving neighbourhoods, has begun secondary patrolling as back-up to the NOPD. As I walked to the other end of the block during the police action yesterday, I saw two more Hummers, one going each way on Elysian Fields. The neighbourhood was surrounded. Again.

When I arrived back home one of the soldiers came over and asked me for identification, then questioned me as to where I live. I told him and he took notes, though I had no ID. I had been planning on gardening in my front yard, you see, and was unprepared to pass military checkpoints.

I asked what was happening and he said that this time most of the dealers had fled before they had arrived, but that they were now planning on leaving stake-outs unobtrusively throughout the neighbourhood for the next week, and would catch anyone who returned.

I saw one man, a habitual drunkard and drug-user born and raised in the neighbourhood, glaring at me from his stoop as I spoke to the soldier. Here is a parasitic creature who has actually been in his element since Katrina, openly selling goods looted from the nearby shoe store on the street in the post-storm weeks. That business also has not reopened. This fellow was happily in his element with the dealers and thieves who had begun to congregate at our intersection, and as I looked up and saw him staring at me, he plainly mouthed the words: "You just wait."

I point to him, and then to the Humvee and its occupants.

These soldiers are ready to commit insecticide.

I want the roaches to know that.

So, you ask, just what is this "mojo?"

The precious gifts of life are fragile in post-Katrina New Orleans.
But voodoo still has the power to beat the devil.

Sometimes, for brief moments only, it seems advantageous to live in a place where fear and ignorance can indiscriminately take the upper hand.

Seems two old friends in Los Angeles are getting married, and I want to send them something as a gift—they've both been very generous to me with their friendship and their unselfish introduction of a Looziana boy into the west-coast media community over the years. So I want to send an only-from-New-Orleans and only-from-me gift to celebrate their union. After much rumination I decide I will go to my favorite voodoo shop (the XXX Botanica is literally the Wal-Mart of voodoo paraphernalia) and put together a packet of lucky charms. Surely a New Orleans sort of thing, that. The XXX is out in a bad part of the Faubourg St John area, and a bit of a drive, but I figure that the effort will make it more of a heartfelt gift.

I leave early, eager to put my plans into action. Only as I am driving I do begin to wonder if the shop will even be open. But when I pull up to an expired parking meter a little before 9am, I find that they have already been doing business for several hours—"open early for your spell-casting needs," I suppose.

I walk up and down aisles stacked to the ceiling with mojos of various sorts and I finally settle on buying scented oils, three ready-made potions, a protective powder, an attraction candle and a love-in-marriage candle.

Corazon Accuardito, the owner, comes into the main room from a storage area in back. He carries an armload of small premixed *tisanes* in canvas bags, which I recognise as some of his bestsellers. These are very specifically concocted, everything from "good luck in court" and "taxman stay away" powders to "Black Cat put the hex on them" candles. Corazon is required by law to stamp the word "alleged" on any item that is labelled as to its use, so most are unmarked. But he and his assistant know the Botanica's inventory down to the smallest item. He is happy to see me, gives me a good natured reprimand for coming around so infrequently.

"I've been writing a film script early mornings every day, then teaching school in the afternoon, and at night and on weekends I continue renovating my ancient crumbling house in the Marigny. This has been going on for months on end, with me working like a slave... I haven't gone anywhere or visited anyone," I moan.

"*Pobrecito*. Moving to those privileged upper classes Fidel always talked about. You looking like the corrupted gentry," Corazon replies over his shoulder, still shelving candles. "I order you as a rich landowner to spend lots of money in this poor man's store. I need to make me a bet on a certain east-coast pony. I got a strong feel handling the *Picayune* sports section this morning. Money coming. Sucker money. And in you walk."

"Fine," I say, "since you always make me gamble when I come here anyway."

Corazon laughs, considering this the appropriate response between men of *machismo*, and goes back to business restocking and mumbling to himself as he handles his wares.

A cash-register magic man

Corazon is well known as most powerful among the *traiteurs* of New Orleans. He controls much of the mojo hardware on both the east and west bank of the river, and has become a force in both the African/Creole voodoo and the Latin Santeria crowds. He and I have been buddies for over a decade, for no known reason. We have come to know each other's weaknesses well and both delight in them. We are quite similar in general approach to life, though very different in the specifics of how we deal with it. I describe the man to friends as a loyal and protective though distant friend, a "nice fellow," if occasionally a little scary. We have met infrequently over the past years while partying at Cuban exile nightclubs and checking out the leg at Central American festivals.

Accuardito migrated to New Orleans from Miami because his magic was considered too dark for the Florida crowd. He told me that the people there gave him respect, but were too frightened of his reputation to actually bring him their custom. Even the parish priests in Little Havana refused to hear his confession. So he moved to New Orleans, a town well known as an old world village where the blackest of arts seems an everyday matter, and where the XXX Botanica now sits prosperously jowl-to-jowl with a steakhouse in which every local politician eats at least once a week.

I go back for a final vial of "come-to-me" oil. I know that the items I bought in the shop are really only trinkets unless I get them touched and the proper words said over them.

This is the way the "serious" hoodoo community that lives with the Botanica at its centre protects itself from *las touristas*, whether they are local or from out of town, disrespectful people who walk in the door laughing to buy pretty candles or bright orange spirit floor-wash. The shop takes their money, hands them their souvenirs, and shows them the door. For real folks it's different. The dark-visaged woman at the cash register engages her customer's eyes for a moment, then passes her hands eloquently over each item as she rings it up. And energy flows into the piece.

I figure that since Corazon is there, I'd get the master himself to charge the psychic batteries of my gift, and make it really special.

Twenty bucks, he asks for his blessing. He says he is broke but that his hunch on the ten-to-one pony truly needs a long-shot investment. At this point in my continuing house reconstruction, twenty bucks translates to me as six two-by-fours less for my downstairs bathroom wall. Again, I figure it's worth the money to make the offering right. I give the *traiteur* the cash. Corazon hoos and hahs and mumboes and jumboes and waggles his hands and puts oil on the candles and touches them with holy cards of the African saints.

These are really cast-off second-hand holy cards of Catholic saints. Corazon buys the yellowing pieces of printed cardboard at a discount from a religious clearing house in Texas, and now is forming the foundation of the Accuarditos' next-generation cottage industry. Corazon's 7-year-old son is president and CEO, his main job currently consisting of darkening beatific faces each night after he does his math homework. *El Presidente* is paid three cents a tan.

With their heightened colour, the religious figures receive different names, each a remnant of the century old half-remembered religions of freed slaves. Almost everyone who comes into the XXX is still a very devout practicing Catholic. The duality of beliefs never seems to worry, or even occur, to them. It also does not bother Corazon's cash register.

Or his concentration on blessing my purchases. Finally, he says *"Finito."* I hand him the $20 bill, and the equine seer goes to the phone to call his bookie and place the bet.

Me, I wave goodbye, carry my newly-powered-up purchases back to the car, and drive back home to the Marigny, a few blocks from the Mississippi River.

Because you're mine

I find a Louisiana Creole tomato-box (just emptied of the last of its bounty only a few days ago, the season now sadly ending), and I pad the inside of the box with fragrant herbs from the back yard, potent fresh rosemary, germander and comfrey, dried St John's Wort and swamp mint. Then I put in Corazon's candles and bottles and cover them with more herbs and pennies with black Xs painted on them. Uncrossing signs are protection, and reflect the evil eye, Corazon told me, that's why he's got three on his store. I then add gold-painted chicken bones (doesn't every household keep a stock of these useful items?), and skull-and-crossbones-stamped good-luck cards. I figure that this is one gift that won't be duplicated, even at a Hollywood wedding.

I seal the whole thing up with bubble wrap, put on holographic party paper, then another layer of plain brown paper and shipping tape. I call an express delivery service to come and get it—I have a commercial account that makes that little pick-up convenience free—and I put a note on my front door, saying that the package is hidden behind the large potted palm on the porch.

I hide it there because I can't hear the doorbell from the small cottage behind the house, where I toil away in my hodge-podge of a video-editing suite. So, the package gets hidden behind the palm.

An hour later, I go outside to see if the courier has come by yet, and there, right where I left the package, is the outer wrapping and the shipping label, crumpled and torn. No box inside. I call the express company to see if the courier simply changed the wrapping—they some-times think my work is not sturdy enough for shipping—and no, they say, the courier has not yet been in my area. Won't be until 6.30pm. He's running late.

My gift has been stolen.

Not only that, but the thief was brazen enough to stand on my porch for the time it took to unwrap it and see the brightly coloured paper inside, then take off the outer brown paper and shipping label in one piece and tauntingly leave it right where the package was originally hidden. All this up on my raised porch, at noon, and in full view of the entire neighbourhood.

I am bummed. Seriously angry.

I yell for a few minutes at the walls. This has been a none-too-hospitable week, what with the frustrating logistics of old-house manual labour and attendant economic hassles, and the theft really tops it off. Then I decide that I won't let some jerk get the best of me. That I'll drive back across town to the Botanica and get exactly the same things, come back and package it and still make the 6.30 pickup. I will not be defeated.

But as I walk out the door I see a neighbour a few doors south out on the sidewalk sweeping, and I figure she might have seen the culprit who stole my package. I walk over and ask her, but no, she's been working on her front garden for over an hour and no one has passed her way except two other neighbours we both know well. I trudge back to the car, and then on an impulse continue north to the corner of the block, and look east, then west.

West. There in the middle of the block on the sidewalk, is the decorative inner wrapping-paper. I walk down, pick it up, and inspect it. It has been torn off in a single piece just like the outer wrapping. I see the young children of a Vietnamese couple I know, a pair of sweet kids, playing on the *banquette* across the street, and I walk over to ask if they've seen anyone. They tell me they just came outside and no one has passed by them since then, but that they had heard a commotion outside about half an hour earlier.

I am energised. I walk a few doors further to the corner hardware store, go inside and ask the owner if he's heard or seen anything. He says that he heard yelling and screaming, too, but that when he looked outside expecting to see someone being stabbed to death, all he saw were two young teenaged gang-sorts running toward Rampart Street, "hollering like the devil was after them."

I go back outside and look north up Elysian Fields Avenue.

And I see it. There, about ten feet from the intersection, is the tomato-box. I run over and pick it up. It is barely damaged at all. The top bubble wrap has just been pulled back, exposing all the mojo signs, herbs, bones. And the evil-eye-protection pennies.

The thieves thought they had robbed a hoodoo man.

Word has spread quickly. The theft occurred Thursday. Yesterday, Friday, as people walked from that northerly neighbourhood past my house on their way to the Royal Street bus-stop, every single person stepped quickly to the other side of the street rather than pass directly in front of my door, and the passersby only glanced back obliquely once they had passed.

Most crossed themselves before and after looking.

I called to see if Corazon's horse won. It had, and handily. I was invited to drop by the shop the next day for lunch. Señora Accuardito, in a fit of gratitude to Santa Barbara's financial gift (the Señora was receiving a newer used washing-machine as a result of the long-shot), was cooking her husband a rather massive noonday repast. Corazon was to receive a third of the food, and I (as the original provider of the cash) was awarded the second portion.

The remainder was to be placed at the feet of the large plaster Santa Barbara that decorates the counter at the *Tres Equis.*

Gracias, Santa Barbara, gracias para los todos.

For everything. Including lunch.

Hell hath no fury: Katrina's weight

New Orleans a year after Katrina remains a city of multiple distresses and defiant hope.

The destruction laid upon New Orleans in the wake of hurricane Katrina on 29 August 2005 and subsequent days was a direct result of women's lib.

The historical facts speak for themselves. The French explorer Iberville first came ashore on Mardi Gras Day 1696, and promptly started querying local braves of the Houmas, Chittimacha and Choctaw tribes about a suitable place for a long-term encampment. He gave the native men mirrors and cheap trinkets, and in return generally received a great deal of contrary and confused male-bonding-style speculation. That is, until 1718 [1], when he took the Indian medicine men's finally-proffered advice for a permanent settlement and erected his first log structures in a suspiciously marshy-looking bend in the Mississippi river.

It was only when the rainy season set in that he discovered he had spent a goodly part of a year building in a flood plain, and would eventually need to construct levees in order to live there year-round.

Only then did he wonder why the Indians had sent him to such an obviously inappropriate place.

The problem was that manly Iberville, who could cross vast oceans with only the aid of primitive navigational gear, who could fight alligators and bears with single-shot muskets and a sword, this brave and intelligent man was not at all the most observant sort when it came to social situations.

He had never noticed the tall, striking, and handsome women who were seriously and silently scowling in the shadows of the braves with whom he negotiated. The Frenchman figured *les femmes indiennes* to be nothing more than a close kin of what he considered as the traditional, chronically disgruntled, though rather intimidating, French wives. The latter were rumoured to be one of the reasons he himself stayed onboard his ship for years at a time. He did not envy their husbands.

Iberville was wrong. Badly, sorely wrong. The tribes he had met were predominantly *matriarchal*, and the regal women were the chiefs. They were not happy to be ignored and denigrated. They were insulted and angered at being dismissed by the wigged and powdered white man. When the female chiefs finally instructed their subservient tribesmen to point to a future site for New Orleans, Iberville would again not discern where the giggles and repressed guffaws were originating, and who was laughing about what.

And thus New Orleans was founded on a practical joke perpetrated by scorned women.

A wound still raw

These days the joke just ain't funny any more. The pressure of a civilisation gone awry from the long-term destruction that started with wind and water [2], and continues with a breakdown of humanity, has ripped many a good man and woman from their tenuous holds on sanity. The city's suicide rate is through the roof, the mental-health facilities almost non-existent, and many older residents who could not physically or emotionally stand the strain of life as a refugee have literally given up and died while attempting to return.

Those who have returned and stayed bear The Weight. The Weight of Daily Living in a town with widespread destruction, a struggling infrastructure, and the constant and painful emotional wounds caused by bureaucratic bunglings of government and no-bid commerce as these forces supposedly [3] try to help us right our lives.

We have hundreds of armed national guardsmen roaming our streets in Humvees and a hoard of Louisiana state police bunked in town, these to supplement a New Orleans police force (NOPD) that is not that much smaller than before the hurricane. These inflated numbers of law-enforcement officials are here to keep a hold on a population [4] less than a third its pre-storm size. In July 2006, despite this double-patrolling of a third the people, we had twenty-one murders, as opposed to twenty-two in the same month a year earlier.

Which means the murder rate per thousand had tripled.

Last weekend was a prime example of the bedlam.

On Friday, two national guardsmen were arrested for stopping cars randomly and then stealing all the money from the drivers' wallets when they were supposedly examining their IDs.

On Saturday morning, in the destroyed lower ninth ward, which is surrounded and patrolled by the same national guard, someone drove onto a work site and brazenly stole two large-tracked bulldozers. The perpetrators had to have a flat-bed truck and take at least an hour to load the massive dozers onto their vehicle, chain them down, and drive out of the area. To compound the insult, the equipment was stolen from the construction site for a memorial dedicated to the people who died in that neighbourhood on 29-30 August 2005 [5], poor people drowned first by floodwaters and now by irony.

On Saturday night, in a more personally affective event, three men walked into Mimi's in the Marigny, two blocks from my home, pulled a gun and robbed the bar/restaurant and ten patrons. Many of them were my neighbours: artists, carpenters, day-labourers and a magician. Threatening their lives if anyone moved or spoke. This, in spite of a video surveillance system and door-buzzer locks.

Other than the two national guardsmen, there have been no arrests.

Under this sort of onslaught, it is hard not to give up. I personally have lost more acquaintances post-K than in the storm. Then I am told the story of John McCusker, read reports of his arrest, and drop another notch into anxiety myself.

John stayed through the horror of the city's darkest days, working at documenting the worst disaster in American history and the personal agonies undergone by so many individuals.

The pictures may have emptied from his cameras into digital storage, but the images never seem to have left his mind.

He was a wonderfully talented photographer for the *New Orleans Times-Picayune* [6], like me was a long-time jazz enthusiast (though he was even more proactive in the music community), was an alumnus and newspaper editor from Loyola University (where I teach), and was at the end of the day a true family man. He was a husband and father locked into the community, whose wife also worked at the paper, whose kids attended New Orleans schools, and whose home and life were totally wrecked by Katrina. There are online interviews with John as he described his descent [7] into hell, the price he was paying for life under The Weight.

Then last week while all this other mayhem was roaring on, he himself dropped into the inferno. Lost it. Pulled over for erratic driving, he fought officers, then begged to be killed, and when incredibly restrained NOPD officers refused, he tried to crush them with his vehicle. They eventually tasered him into submission without endangering his life.

Just reading the reports would have broken New Orleans's collective heart, had the scarred old organ any more capacity for such a feeling.

Since then, according to reports, John has begun finding his way back from the edge, positively affected by how so many people have been touched by his story and have tried to help him, in any way they can.

And because of his trauma, more outsiders are beginning to realise what a toll [8] The Weight continues to take every day on the stressed and pressured few who continue to try and deny the city any further slide into chaos.

John McCusker's breakdown was made all the more meaningful when one of his photos appeared on the cover of last Friday's *Lagniappe* section in the paper, the arts and entertainment section. The term *lagniappe* is part of the old New Orleans vernacular—after buying some tomatoes and greens, a regular customer at a French Market stand would always receive an extra ripe banana or two, and maybe an apple, from the fruit vendor for the buyer's continued custom. It was a way of saying "thanks for helping me stay alive" from the seller. This giving of a "little something extra" is one of the building-blocks [9] of what was, and hopefully remains, the city's uniquely human culture.

So, what if this community was founded on a bad joke, and so what if the anniversary of Katrina is being mined by politicians [10] and media for money and emotion like it is the punchline of yet another, even worse, gag?

In the end we have the final laugh. Because we intend to make it work.

We will, John. We will. Because we know how to take a joke, and a little *lagniappe*, and make something good out of it.

URLS

[1] www.oup.com/us/catalog/general/subject/HistoryAmerican/Southern/?view=usa&ci=9780195301366
[2] today.reuters.com/news/articlenews.aspx?type=domesticNews&storyID=2006-08-29T120451Z_01_N27437748_RTRUKOC_0_US-WEATHER-HURRICANES-DESIGN.xml
[3] www.newhousenews.com/archive/mowbray082806.html
[4] www.theglobeandmail.com/servlet/story/RTGAM.20060826.wxxneworleans26/BNStory/International/home
[5] www.cbc.ca/news/background/katrina/katrina_timeline.html
[6] www.nola.com/t-p/
[7] www.theglobeandmail.com/servlet/story/RTGAM.20060829.wxneworleans29/BNStory/International/home
[8] www.iht.com/articles/2006/08/28/opinion/edbosworth.php
[9] www.nola.com/newslogs/tpupdates/index.ssf?/mtlogs/nola_tpupdates/archives/2006_08_26.html#176450
[10] www.voanews.com/english/2006-08-29-voa23.cfm

Life as a remainder

It's life, love and home, but a year after Katrina is it time to look beyond New Orleans?

Ok, I admit it.

I sleep with a 10-year-old boy every night. Or at least I have up until now.

That is not the reason my partner may well be leaving.

Or maybe it is.

The last few weeks she has talked increasingly about the options for where she is moving. *Where*, not *if*. It is only a matter of time before she finds something she can do, even something other than her successful practice of a law based on Napoleonic Code, somewhere, anywhere, other than New Orleans.

Even before Katrina, she always said the only reason she stayed here was my refusal to even discuss living anywhere else. And so, for twenty-four years this industrious Midwestern Girl has put up with a raucous Deep South Boy & his Deep South City. Over that time she has learned how to deal with my antics, but she has never really made her peace with New Orleans, in spite of her love of its food and music and deep heart-warming culture.

During her childhood years she and her parents and five sisters were nomadic wanderers of the American Great Plains, army folks moving frequently through a progression of faceless, flat towns and military installations in Nebraska and Missouri. She could never quite fathom my consummate need to nest, especially here. Still, there was an entirely new setting for life every few years, and the changing environments set a pattern of life that would follow her into adulthood. She likes to move about.

Besides, she would say, *what perverse motivation could you possibly have for dropping permanent roots at the swamp-gagged mouth of the Mississippi, amidst the humidity, snakes and impolite drag queens?*

Even when I showed her the pictures of my parents on their French Quarter honeymoon night in 1947, toasting each other at the Old Absinthe Bar on Bourbon Street, smiling wryly before bedding down at the luxurious Monteleone Hotel around the corner, she still would ask the question.

Why?

I tell her the other end of the honeymoon story, that they leave New Orleans, go to the casinos on the Mississippi Gulf Coast, lose all their money, and end up spending the rest of their honeymoon on lumpy single cots back in the city at the Lee Circle Y, a post-war youth hostel.

And this is romantic?

How even when they get their dream, a tiny chain of weekly newspapers in central Louisiana, they always load up the kids for a week every summer and come back downriver to the crescent city. To get their creative energy back.

So?

I tell her of college weekends in burlesque houses, of three-piece bump & grind jazz bands sprayed with soap suds by the swirling buttocks of Linda "the champagne girl" Brigette in a six-foot champagne glass, of the many mistakes of Mardi Gras, of the survival of hurricane Audrey in 1955 and especially hurricane Betsy in 1965, during my first week away from home at university. A dorm room with three feet of water and a like number of cases of beer. I tell her all those things. The roots are here, I tell her. They run too deep. I can't leave.

I don't get it.

But she lets me slide and stays. This is a good person. A very good person, with a great heart and a seemingly infinite capacity to forgive.

Twenty-three years of a relationship pass.

Comes The Storm.

Another year passes, and finally, unequivocally, the price of living in this city has become too high for her. It seems that every single person who returned to stay these last twelve months has been chronically dogged by constant depression and lingering physical maladies, sometimes the pain rising to life-threatening levels. She has been no exception, but has bravely forged on. Until now.

Now, I fear—no, I know—that after two decades of forbearance, I alone am no longer reason enough for her continuing to live here.

I do not blame her.

No matter what people say of the impossibility of my emigration, or even their own—"I would never leave." "I and the place where I live are one and the same creature"—the fact is that the thought of moving elsewhere never leaves my mind these days.

I feel this is a constant with each and every person who remains.

And yet we do remain.

Not here yet

But now, just yesterday morning, my big grey tabby starts limping and acting funny. Not in pain, but dazed and dizzy. I pick him up to find that he has a lump on his right shoulder that wasn't there two days ago. I think maybe he has dislocated his shoulder in one of his house-defense fights. I take him to the vet. No dislocation, they say. Rather, a rapidly expanding sarcoma. Biopsy immediately, they say. Incurable cancer likely.

Ten-year-old Koko has spent every night of his life on my bed, guarding me while I sleep, every night since I first found the tiny four-week-old grey ball of fur at the animal shelter sitting in a bowl of cat chow, guarding it. Last year, he went along with my decision and evacuated with me—a horrible seventeen-hour nightmare in a tiny VW—and never lost the faith for seven weeks as a refugee, until I could bring him back to the city.

New Orleans in general, and everything inside the old cast-iron fence at 725 rue Marigny in specific, belongs to him, and he to it.

He returned in October 2005. It is now September 2006.

An early-morning phone call today predicts Koko to be dead within eight weeks.

He is the second of our three cats to be diagnosed with a malignant cancer in just the last three months. Neither were ever sick pre-K. I do not think about this.

Like I try not to think about the future. It is not here yet.

I look at my parents' picture.

I remain.

At least until Happy Hour, eh?

Long life lines

New Orleans meets Beirut in Las Vegas and discovers solidarity in the embrace of life.

I was directing four days of high-definition television broadcasts at the National Association of Broadcasters annual show [1] in Las Vegas last spring when I suddenly encountered more Lebanese nationals than I had ever met before.

Apart, that is, from one of my father's family reunions.

In spite of three days' journey, missed planes and sweaty bus rides, the twenty student interns from the American University of Beirut (it is known as AUB [2]) television-studies programme were excited and ready to work. They started calling me by what I took to be an Arabic pronunciation of my surname and, when they asked its origins, were delighted to discover my lineage. Even the announcement of my seriously Irish mother did not seem to deter their tagging me "the Lebanese director."

I didn't mind. Actually I found it rather charming and romantic, being identified with a city that just forty years ago was a renowned traditional Mediterranean destination [3] for vacation and commerce, a place dubbed in financial circles as the "Geneva of the east." In spite of the intervening devastation of political violence, I was told that the city had finally come again into its own long-held course of peace and prosperity, and that in 2006 AUB itself was actually celebrating the 140th year of its founding, with 7,000 students coming to Beirut from over sixty countries.

The kids' descriptions of their people, school and homes seem to indicate that the heydays were indeed possibly returning, and from my distant vantage-point of an over-decorated Nevada hotel room in April 2006, their city sounded to be thriving again.

Unlike my own.

They knew about the storm, and each of the kids repeatedly demanded such detailed descriptions of the devastation of New Orleans [4] that I finally had to insist that they not ask me anything further. It was all too painful and raw. They apologised and invariably said they empathised with my hometown, thinking it, like Beirut, a similar anomaly in its own country—both cities considered by their brethren talented but unmannered outcasts. New Orleans and Beirut both just had too much fun for the stiff suits and politicians, they told me, and that is why they choose to ignore our plight, the government hoping we'll just go away.

They were young and from the other side of the world, but they were damned close to the heart of the problem.

I spent some time during the week I worked with those students reflecting on my own typically diverse American lineage, my mother's people arriving from western Europe some two centuries ago, and my father's mother and father disembarking at Ellis Island [5] in New York harbour just over a century later, after visa waits in southern France and Havana.

My generation has been thoroughly Americanised, and I do not really know much about my parents' peoples. Though, besides the exuberant youth I witnessed in Vegas, I have found that longevity seems a defining trait of the Lebanese I have known. My father—who still goes to work daily in his print shop as he approaches his 93d birthday—has long told the tale, corroborated by my grandmother, of his own great-grandfather. After almost a century, the family still mourned a vital man cut down in his prime, a dedicated worker, and a moderately talented recreational dancer, forced into an early and permanent retirement when a crate fell on him as he went about his job as harbourmaster of Beirut.

At the time of the accident, great-great-grandpapa was 102 years old, still drawing a weekly paycheque. My grandmother could not remember if the family received a workman's compensation settlement, but thought that, somewhere, she still had the gold watch the harbor authority awarded in lieu of the old man's continued existence.

I found this propensity for a long active life a comforting legacy from my father, and enjoyed this accidental reawakening of interest in his family's place of origin. Through the following summer, I watched the places the students had mentioned to me on the internet, watched via live webcams as the arts scene and sidewalk cafe neighborhoods of Beirut expanded. I was even considering entering my new film in the DocuDays film festival [6] at the American University, as an excuse to visit the country, the students and teachers I had met in Vegas for the first time. Yet another rootless American's fascination with roots.

Then came Beirut's [7] own hurricane.

Tanks and bombs and rockets rained down on the city from 12 July until 14 August, and again the suits, the people in charge of the killing, ignored the devastation [8] and deaths of thousands of innocent individuals, people whose politics were never deeper than which fish-market they would visit for the evening meal. My new acquaintances from AUB were caught in a bloody vise. Their existence was threatened by strangers' distorted sense of national pride.

I tried unsuccessfully to get in communication with the university. I watched the news for familiar faces. I saw the webcams go down. I saw two of the student cafes I had been told were near the university completely demolished. I began to remember their sincere condolences on the damage done to my city's heart, and now reflected on their own losses.

It was all too familiar.

But they are long-lived, these Lebanese. I suspect they will outlive the hatred and discord and misguided nationalists on all sides. This past week, on 26 September, 1,900 new enrollees signed up to join the students already in place, and the school reopened at very close to its pre-hostilities strength.

The webcams are coming back online. The cafes putting up new doors.

Welcome back, my friends.

As a newly-minted survivor myself, I can only offer the family adage.

If after a century of life my grizzled ancestor could leave this world on his own terms, working happily and dancing about the docks of Beirut without a worry as to the outside world, then I absolutely know for a fact that fun is still possible, in *both* our towns.

And joy certainly does aggravate those suits.

URLS

[1] www.nabshow.com/nab2006/
[2] www.aub.edu.lb/about/
[3] www.opendemocracy.net/conflict-middle_east_politics/riviera_citadel_3841.jsp
[4] www.opendemocracy.net/debates/article.jsp?id=6&debateId=129&articleId=2811
[5] www.ellisisland.com/ellis_home.html
[6] www.docudays.com/
[7] www.opendemocracy.net/conflict-middle_east_politics/beirut_3792.jsp
[8] www.opendemocracy.net/conflict-middle_east_politics/lebanon_lecarre_3856.jsp

Friday the thirteenth

New Orleans does funerals like nowhere else on earth.

Over dinner conversation the other night, in the middle of yet another post-K discussion of mortality, somehow arose the subject of "favourite funerals". This topic is savored in the culture that is New Orleans, a place where such ceremonies celebrate life, rather than death.

I remember my own personal favourite, from just a very few years back.

Ernest Kador Jr, aka "Ernie K-Doe", who sang 1961's number-one hit "Mother-in-Law", and half a dozen other top-ten hits, passed away in the same New Orleans hospital in which he was born. Big Charity, they called it, to differentiate it from the smaller satellites in Huey Long's health system for the poor. Pre-K, the sprawling beige stone structure occupied more than three blocks of prime real estate downtown, on Tulane Avenue.

Crescent City funeral arrangers gathered K-Doe's remains from Big Charity quickly, but needed eight days to get ready for such a monu- mental event as sending Ernie on, even though the R & B singer died practically penniless. His funeral was scheduled to cross the noon hours of Friday the thirteenth, in the largest and grandest historic setting in the city—the front ballroom of Gallier Hall, the antebellum mayor's quarters on St Charles Avenue.

This city always plays against tradition, and for many here, including myself, the thirteenth is considered very auspicious and lucky.

I sign the guestbook at a table manned by old-line members of the New Orleans music family. A lovely Creole woman of a decade's acquain- tance winks at me and reaches under the table to discreetly draw out and present me with me a booklet. As always, there is more to any situation in this town than originally meets the eye: funeral organisers have printed a special-edition color keepsake funeral programme for music's inner community which they keep out of sight and distribute sparingly—this as opposed to the black & white xerox copy still gener- ously handed out to the massive general crowds. Through the progress of the day my commemorative copy is to become sweaty and distressed. However, I consider that a positive attribute, in the same way a well- worn book shows it has often given comfort.

Just beyond the registration table, an old man walks about with an air of authority wearing an official red "Usher" ribbon. The funeral is already in progress as he directs mourners to bathrooms and overflow chambers. Otherwise, he has no idea of where he is—the gentleman has dressed for the services with his suit completely inside out, both coat and pants. Underneath he wears a beautifully starched and ironed white shirt. He disappears after about an hour, then shows up later as the bands start to play. This time he is in the saddle of a bicycle covered in multicoloured propellers, riding up and down in front of the thousands of people gathered outside of Gallier Hall who can't fit into the building.

Inside an absolutely typical New Orleans scene occurs during the funeral itself. The first hour of testimonials, performance, and prayers happen exactly on time as described in programme, a remarkable feat for this city. But then, right as the formal eulogy is to begin, a young man pushes his way to the front of room, and uninvited, literally grabs a mike away from the elderly master of ceremonies. The intruder is wearing a red jacket that looks at least two sizes two big, over a white collarless shirt. He is well-groomed, though there is something off-kilter and huckster-ish about him.

"Let me introduce myself", he announces, "I am Ernest Kador's nephew. I am a Baptist preacher, and Mr K-Doe often sought my advice. I used to sing for him, as I will for you now", and begins to sing "I'm Gonna Let It Shine". He is quite good and quickly steals the show—it is suddenly a show—bellowing lyrics and calling to a heavenly reward with a grand resonant voice, turning each line into a preacher's invocation of his Lord. But after five minutes, the family on the podium begin to get restless. No one actually seems to recognise the man, and in spite of gentle hints and ushers reaching for his mike, he resists and won't stop his act.

People in the audience are oblivious to the situation, everyone on their feet, eyes closed, hands raised over their heads.

"He'p me, Jesus!"

"Good gawd awmighty!"

"Brother K-Doe!"

A mighty and abundant joy is come to Gallier Hall.

The older preachers onstage, including the reverend who was just about to deliver the eulogy, are useless—their own congregations have not prepared them to deal with someone so aggressive. It takes JazzFest gospel producer Sherman Washington to intercede. Quadruple bypass or no, he stands up, ever the stalwart guide through potential tragedies, yells to the musicians and points a hard finger at the singer, who instantly stops and disappears from the room. He is to be found shortly afterwards in the hallway outside distributing business cards.

Then comes the actual eulogy. The poor old gent begins slowly and with a powerful voice, an excellent orator in his own right, but he never has a chance after what has just occurred. A moment before we were in the midst of a religious riot. Now the room is deathly still with the slow rhythmic bass cadence of his speech.

Muttering begins quietly at first, then conversation increases, and before a minute has passed the room is ignoring the eulogy and talking about what is to be served at the repast.

Sherman is needed again. He stands and calls for "quiet in the hall", yelling loudly right over top of the dead body in the casket. I expect Ernie to get up and holler back "Tain't It the Truth" in response.

The dearly departed is wearing his "Emperor of the Universe" suit, complete with foot-tall crown and his sceptre. Supposedly he legally changed his name to become the Emperor a few years back, just to get the proper respect. With the new wig and crown the 5'7" K-Doe is 6'8". The funeral directors have to drastically adjust his crown to close the coffin completely. Ernie knew about displays.

As does his wife. For a week Antoinette and cousin Tee Eva have had an altar set up in front of the Mother-in-Law Lounge on Claiborne Avenue. People have been piling the strangest memorabilia on it for the last eight days. When I drove by yesterday afternoon I saw what looked like a toilet lid that had been festooned with dozens of plastic flowers and fashioned into a lucky-horseshoe funeral wreath. The inscription, K-Doe's life-long evocation of the R & B ghosts, is applied with a felt-tip marker. I am not sure it is entirely appropriate upon the occasion of a death, but it is true to the man. The wreath reads: "Burn, K-Doe, burn!", which was K-Doe's own invocation to crowds when he knew he really had them working.

Antoinette also made the papers yesterday by donating the costumes she made for herself and K-Doe and Eva to the state's Jazz Museum. The group Friends of New Orleans Cemeteries had named K-Doe the Grand Marshal of its Mourning Glory Ball this year, and honored Ernie and Antoinette with one of its "Gravie" awards for "inventing the custom of dressing to match the deceased at a funeral."

It's true. Originally Antoinette had made a very fancy new suit for another deceased musician's body, and K-Doe liked the way the corpse looked in the suit so much that he asked his wife to sew the whole family outfits just like the one on the gent in the coffin. Then K-Doe, wife and cousin wore them to the funeral, and the mourners' outfits perfectly complemented the dead man's.

She's made Ernie another spangled suit for his own casket today, plus bought him a new and even bigger wig, complements of a fund fans started taking up the very night of his death.

Antoinette had urged everyone to costume for her husband's funeral. "No black," she'd announced in the newspapers. Across her own white dress, she wore her "Empress Antoinette" sash from her co-reign with her husband as the regal honourees of the Krewe du Vieux parade this past Mardi Gras.

Everyone else took her clothing pronouncement seriously. Musicians Johnny Angel & Coco Robicheaux, close friends of K-Doe's, dressed in striking colors, only to be stuck in back room watching services on an overflow monitor. They couldn't get into the jammed main room, even though Coco has flown all the way back in from Colorado to pay his respects. K-Doe sang at Coco's wedding only a month earlier. I attended the gigantic party at the legendary Rosy's Bar uptown, just to see the two warbling on the same stage, and because I loves them boys.

Almost time to go now. Outside, ten matched police Harleys are parked in front of the procession. Each one is emblazoned with the new NOPD logo on tanks and windshield—a blue down-pouring crescent with matching star nestled underneath, both supported by golden wings. I sat staring at them for some time—I don't think you could find a more appropriate symbol for this funeral.

A sea of black umbrellas and multicoloured parasols are already bobbing to the music for the "second-line", the group that forms the second line of mourners behind the family. Held overhead, the umbrellas also offer some limited protection from the summer sun. The brick street is incredibly heat-intensive, but folks are already dancing, waiting for the coffin to come out.

This is a wonderfully mixed and harmonious crowd. Half a block away from the door where K-Doe will emerge, two elderly women, one white, one black, sit on a concrete wall talking about their idol, and what he meant to their lives. The white woman has her hair full of glitter. The black woman is wearing a cheerleader outfit and carrying a four-foot-tall monkey hand-puppet. Antoinette will be pleased when she passes.

The police have lined the start-up formation to go east, backwards down St Charles Avenue to Poydras street. As you may have noticed, the simplest acts in New Orleans often become charged, deeper, because of the way disparate pieces of our world accidentally come together. This now happens. The air becomes goosebump-filled, and then completely eerie.

It's the birds. Electronic birds.

I will explain.

Next door to Gallier Hall where K-Doe lies in state is the United States Reserve Bank. The bank has been having trouble with its parking lot— pigeon problems because of the birds nesting in the huge oak trees there and crapping continually on all the Feds' cars. To keep birds out, they have installed large owl-shaped balloons in the tops of the trees, and have set speakers in trees playing loud hawk screeching and owl hooting. So, when the crowd stops applauding after band plays a funeral dirge, the silence is filled with all these very loud and cacophonous bird noises, right here in the middle of the city.

Not many people know the source, so there are lots of knowing smiles— K-Doe's day was meant to be magic.

The noonday heat gets increasingly murderous. As Ernie is brought out and placed in the horse-drawn hearse, the top-hatted driver has to be given water to keep his spirits—and his dehydrating body—up. The parade begins to move, with the stately singer Wanda Rouzan marching out in front as Grand Marshall. But after only walking two blocks, some older folks make their ways to the sidewalks, laying out in the shade fanning themselves, waving goodbye to hearse with traditional white handkerchiefs, as they know they can go no further. They'll catch up with the party in the air-conditioned confines of Rock 'n Bowl, the bowling alley/concert hall/restaurant where the funeral "repast" will be held.

A monumental traffic-jam forms as the parade moves across Canal street to the St Louis Cemetery No 2, the very historic and ancient cemetery where K-Doe is to be interred. Ironically, this has to do with his work with the Friends of the New Orleans Cemeteries. When Antoinette told "Friend" Anna Ross Twitchell that she had no place to bury her husband, Anna recalled that her daughter Heather had a tomb in St Louis Number 2. It was originally built for Heather's paternal great-great-great-great-great grandfather, Jacques Duval. The family would make room for the K-Doe, and the Cemeteries group would fully restore the tomb and dedicate a bronze plaque on its side to the career and persona of the singer of "Mother-in-Law". Heather, a classical harpist, said it was her way of acknowledging the continuity of the musical family of New Orleans.

Ernest Kador is buried in the same cemetery that contains giants of jazz, like Louis Barbarin and Danny Barker.

I once shot a scene for a jazz film with Danny there, and he had taken me to his uncle Louis' tomb. Barbarin's will left his nephew two things—the royalties from "Bourbon Street Parade", the famous New Orleans traditional jazz tune which he wrote, and ... space in that same tomb in St Louis No 2.

It's that big a deal getting a spot for eternity in St Louis Number Two.

And now the self-described "Charity Hospital Baby", Ernest Kador, also rests there.

Burn, K-Doe, burn.

Heavy mettle report

*The destructive cycle of crime and drug-dealing tests the mettle
of New Orleans residents.*

Fifteen thieves are recently dead nationwide in the United States, and
I, for one, do not mourn them. These were humans whom you could
rightly judge from afar as none-too-scrupled and even less intelligent,
without ever meeting them or assessing them individually.

Please don't judge me too harshly on that seemingly cruel remark.
Not just yet. You see, there is this huge surge in metal prices over the
last months, especially the metal that constitutes the least valuable of
American coins: the penny.

The pilferers were all killed attempting to steal copper.

From live electric lines.

Locally, here in New Orleans [1], the heavy-metal crime wave first
appeared as gangs of construction predators who routinely stripped
both demolished and newly-salvaged family homes of all their water
pipes and electrical conduits.

Then came the week where several churches around the area had the
brass railings leading up their front steps, and any other exterior metal
decoration, ripped from the structure and sold as scrap. One church
in the central business district, the very heart of town had both occur:
its railings were stolen one evening, then the very next night all the
plumbing and wiring were ripped out from under the sanctuary.

Things escalated. Century-old gravesites in historic cemeteries have
been pillaged of hundreds and hundreds of urns. Public-utility trucks
carrying heavy pole wiring, and plumbers with copper pipes, began to
implement security measures. In some cases, carrying guns.

Things have escalated, or descended, even further.

John Scott [2] is a sculptor who has inspired this community for over
forty years, a brilliant and dedicated artist of world caliber and reputation. The last eighteen months were not kind to him. His home and
studio took major floodwater and wind damage during Katrina. He
is ageing, has had multiple major operations on his lungs, and is still
in bad physical shape. Many critics and art historians were already
talking about his artistic legacy, even as he lay alive in the hospital.

And then a week or so ago, the metal thieves broke into the already damaged studio to defile and steal most of his work from the last decade. They torched, hammered and cut up the large welded sculptures and cast bronze statues and carted them away.

They were not electrocuted in the process.

I often speak fondly of Faubourg Marigny, the section of New Orleans in which I have now happily lived into a second decade. In spite of, or maybe because of, its laid-back bohemian nature, the Marigny has been plagued by the ebbs and surges of crime for years. Thugs figure they can zoom into the neighbourhood of artists and blue-collar workers, do what they will, and then rush back into their own enclaves, with little or no risk of being apprehended. They figure we aging residents are too slow to react, too mellow to be armed, too much the 1960s "outlaws" to call police.

Two days ago a young neighbour, a fellow [3] filmmaker and an animator, mother of a 2-year-old child, was murdered as she let the family pet out the back door of her apartment at sunup. Robbery was the supposed motive. Her husband, responding to the gunfire and screams, was also shot repeatedly and left for dead clutching the child in his arms, kneeling over his dead wife. The robber fled, taking nothing for his crime. Police, already investigating another similar but not fatal armed break-in at a B&B just a few doors away, arrived quickly but did not find the suspect, who is speculated to have been going house-to-house down the block, looking for prey.

The wounded husband was a doctor who founded a clinic for the poor, a consummate volunteer who was trying to bring basic medical services to a storm-stressed and impoverished neighborhood. Reportedly, he had not wanted to return to New Orleans, but his wife insisted it was their duty.

He and his surviving child have now fled the city, their lives forever changed.

No one home

The destructive pattern [4] traces back to pre-Katrina days. It remains stubbornly present, and has been increasing dramatically this winter.

With the last months' constant bar and business robberies and daily armed muggings, the governor recently ordered more national-guard troops sent into our streets in armoured Humvees. She sent in more state troopers, and pledged they would stay longer. The mayor promised more NOPD officers would be detailed into our neighborhood to stop the escalating wave of drugs, robberies and murders.

And what were we residents to do? Be vigilant and report criminals, they said. But often we are left to wonder on which side of the law the crime occurs.

One of my neighbours spent two months trying to alert police to a neighbourhood crack house full of armed dealers and prostitutes. These were obviously people new to the city, in town for the lawless ride. She took license numbers and descriptions of the intruders, repeatedly called the fifth district police, our city councilman and the various drug hotlines, only to be constantly told that help "is on the way."

A month and then another passed and no help came. The hookers and dealers [5] and their distributor, often armed, began to get bolder. They would wait until the neighbourhood was quiet during the day and then supplement their vice income by breaking into houses while honest residents were away at work.

You'd think they would have been satisfied with their major pursuit, as the drug business was rampant night and day. At 9am one weekday, I personally witnessed a car pull up to the drop-off house, three riders get out, open the automobile's hood, unscrew the air filter and remove a large bag of white powder. They carried what I assumed was crack directly into the house.

I called the police from my cell to report the drug deal in progress, and told the female officer who answered that a quantity of dope was on the premises with the same armed and dangerous criminals who had been intimidating our neighborhood for weeks. She said she'd "call it in." I stood in plain view of the house and waited twenty minutes. No cops. I called again. I was put on hold. Ten more minutes. No one ever came back on the line. The dealers left to carry on their own due diligence.

Luckily, the neighbor who had started the process was not about to give up. She ran into an eighth district policeman at her dentist's office not long after my encounter. When she told him our story, he said he'd call it in right then and there. But he could not get through either, and began to better understand our situation.

He vowed to follow up, and did. He and his cohorts called me and got the license numbers of the dealers, they interviewed the other neighbors on the street for confirmation and got it, they sent cars to hassle the street-corner crack zombies, and finally raided the house.

So, because of a random dental appointment, the eighth district cops found what for months we had been telling our own district was there—dope, dealers, hookers, money, weapons.

But still the violence [6] and the disdain for humanity persists, like the loss of the young couple: idealists who became victims. Like an elderly artist's life work destroyed, his creative soul ripped into pieces for a few dollars.

And though I can only thank the eighth district officers who took it upon themselves to cross artificial boundaries and help us, I can only wonder at the overall police department's approach.

This is the same government agency which parked a gigantic recreational vehicle, a huge self-propelled mobile home emblazoned as an NOPD "mobile command center" or some such grand title, right in the grassy center of Elysian Fields Avenue at the entrance to the Faubourg Marigny.

It stayed parked there at least a month, leaving on new year's day.

That vehicle could serve as the perfect allegory for most of the department's efforts: it was huge and showy and expensive, and in the course of the four weeks it stood parked in our neighbourhood, there was never, ever, anyone inside.

Still, daily the Bad Guys test our mettle. And we continue to live here.

URLS

[1] www.nola.com/
[2] www.bigeasy.com/new-orleans-arts/
[3] www.jimgabour.com/
[4] www.chron.com/disp/story.mpl/nation/4452333.html
[5] www.jointogether.org/news/headlines/inthenews/2006/post-katrina-new-orleans.html
[6] www.katc.com/Global/story.asp?S=5909434

Mahatma 189

New Orleans is still a city of tiny miracles. Here's the proof.

"You know, Jim-Jim, this non-violence shit really pays."

This from the mouth of the infamous "Mad Dog" Salvatano, semi-retired bookie and gambler extraordinaire.

The setting: happy hour at Tujague's Bar on Decatur street, New Orleans, on a classic spring Monday. I made note of the occasion immediately onto a cocktail napkin. I wanted to research later to see if some heavy-metal planet oozing radiation had slipped from orbit, reasoning that there must be some cause for what I had just heard. Contradiction on such a cosmic scale does often not occur without a substantial prompt.

And The Dog is not known as a master of self-restraint in any portion of his life. Thus, his name. This man was embracing non-violence?

He had more to say.

"Yeah, me and my lady we was watching *Gandhi* last night ..."

I felt another slip in the universe.

"... and there he was in prison ..."

This I knew he could relate to.

"... wearing a uniform with the numbers 189 on the pocket."

OK ...

"So I got up right then and there and drove to the Cracker Barrel Mini-mart and put a buck on the Lotto Quick Pick 3, betting the numbers 1, 8 & 9 ..."

Oh, no.

"I tell the cashier where I got my numbers, and she's cute and laughs. Seems to like me, I mean, but who doesn't? Who can resist The Dog in his prime? Though she has these dimples, which are making me crazy. So I buy us each a beer out the cooler, and we have a little talk about this philosophy stuff. We drink a second beer. Almost no customers, you know, on a Sunday night. Even let me sit behind the counter with her while we was sipping our brews. Very classy dame. I got her number."

"Then I figured I'd go finish the movie and get some more of the scoop, but by the time I get home, this Gandhi guy is dead, and Linda smells somebody else's perfume on me and asks me where I been and isn't any too hot about giving me a recap of the plot."

"I figure it can wait and go to bed. Alone."

"So I get up this morning, look at the paper, and sure enough, there it is: the Quick Pick 3 winning numbers are 189. Natch. I won me five hundred bucks because a dead Indian went to jail in South Africa. I'm gonna watch that movie all the way through tonight. Maybe he sent me some more messages, hunh?"

I added that to my notes. *The Dog looks to Gandhi for messages*, I wrote.

Looking at the wadded, marker-stained cocktail napkin now, I have decided to add the flimsy piece of paper to my mojo altar. It's best to pay attention when these things happen, and I am.

Gandhi probably did, too.

Sirens calling

A monster of drug-fuelled violence is strangling New Orleans.
Police and politicians are nowhere to be seen.

The first gunshots startled me.

It was only 7pm, and usually the mayhem starts much later, the sounds of automatic pistols and assault rifles punctuating the darkness from midnight until about four in the morning. But there they were as I started cooking dinner, *pocketa-pocketa-pock-pock*, then the same metre repeated again.

The sounds of one human trying to render another dead. Not a real appetite stimulant.

Only another hour or two into the evening—I admit it, I was already in bed with a book—the sirens started. There had been none for the first, earlier shooting, and these were different from the usual long wavering wails of the American police car. These were shorter, maybe ten to fifteen seconds, and happened in bursts of six to seven sirens within fifteen minutes, then nothing for an hour, then another set.

I suspect the police were trying to let the Bad Guys know they were in the area, and at the same time both reassure, and not alarm, the real residents.

They woke me up. I was not reassured. I was not alarmed. I was *angry.* Because it has come to this.

New Orleans is now two separate creatures.

One is the same welcoming, bawdy, colourful ageing auntie who brings visitors into her living room and gives them a fine old time of food, music, and genteel decadence.

Then there is the monster—the deadly cash- and dope-fuelled fiend that those of us who live here have to contend with on a daily basis. And she is out of control. The politicians all say they have the answer. They have said that a *number* of times over the last eighteen months, but here we are losing neighbours and friends on a daily basis, a murder a day thus far into 2007.

In an hour I will join with hundreds, maybe thousands, of others and march from all over the community to the steps of city hall, to tell the other face of the monster—the politicians—that we have had enough. That we won't live here if we have to die here, at least not die like this.

Please don't be frightened away. Visitors are safe. They are sacred. They are coddled and protected, even while seated comfortably in the massive air-conditioned tour buses that roll through destroyed neighborhoods on "disaster tours." Make no mistake, we need people to come here, to spend money here, to make us feel that it will eventually be alright. We want you to see how valuable and magic this place really is.

But we also need the world to shame the American government into doing what it was founded to do: protect its citizens with more than hollow sirens in the middle of the night.

This is personal

Forty-one years before Virginia Tech, there was the University of Texas.

"M.J and Mary Gabour, their two sons, and William and Marguerite Lamport were headed up the steps from the 27th floor. They found the door barricaded by a desk. Mark and Mike Gabour pushed the desk away and leaned in the door to see what was going on. Suddenly Charlie rushed at them, spraying them with pellets from his sawed-off shotgun. Mark died instantly. Charlie fired down the stairway at least three more times. Marguerite Lamport was killed; Mary Gabour was critically wounded, as was her son Mike. They would lay where they fell for more than an hour."

Marlee MacLeod [1], *Charles Whitman: The Texas Tower Sniper* (account of University of Texas tower massacre, 1 August 1966)

I remember when the word came in. I was home from school for the summer, doing full-time manual labor at my family's small weekly newspaper in central Louisiana. The white concrete was hot that day on *Boeuf Trace*, "Cattle Trail" in Cajun French [2], which was the name of our recently-paved street, running for a mile along palmetto-filled pastures. We were home for an afternoon meal when the heavy old black telephone receiver began ringing metallically in the kitchen. Maybe I sensed something, knew it wasn't one of my buds, because I did not rush the phone as usual.

My father took the call.

He was standing at first. I watched the pale, disbelieving look grow on his face as he slowly and carefully sat on the kitchen stool, the phone poised a few inches from his ear, stopping to stare at it every few seconds like it was something horrible, something foul.

He listened to the voice, grew paler. Held to the windowsill like he was dizzy. I stood a few feet away and watched silently. Not wanting to intrude. Something was happening here, something was being told to my father. Something bad.

I do not remember who was on the phone, who called us first. But the voice told my father that his sister Marguerite Gabour Lamport and his brother's son Mark Gabour were dead. His sister-in-law Mary Francis and our cousin Mike were critically wounded. His brother MJ was tending them, but it was not known if they would survive.

Mike, a cadet at the United States air force academy, lived but his legs had been ruined forever from the shotgun blasts [3]. His mother would be paralysed from the neck down for the rest of her life.

They had been on a tour of the University of Texas tower [4]. Where my two vacationing young brothers had also been, exactly one week before, taken there by the same Lamports, who were all the family's favorite couple.

Only a few days later the cover of *Time* magazine held a heart-wrenching picture of our Uncle Bill walking in a trance alongside a stretcher that held Aunt Margie, her body covered by a bloody sheet. Uncle Bill, himself spattered with his wife's blood, was still holding his wife's hand as the attendants carried her to the waiting hearse. I cried when I saw it. We all did.

Our family was changed forever.

We seldom speak of it these days.

We never speak of it.

And I must apologise to my father and to my extended family if they see this article and think I should not have brought it up again. If I made us all hurt again.

But this is personal.

Today, here in New Orleans, which has seen its share of smaller single-event massacres (the Howard Johnson sniper, new-year's eve 1972), but retains a pattern of more regular ongoing bloodshed, a letter to the editor was published in the *Times-Picayune* [5] in the aftermath of the Virginia Tech killings [6] on 16 April 2007.

A "Professor of Law" at Southern University, a man named MR Franks, wrote the letter, published under the title, "Shooting back could save lives." As a closing paragraph he wrote:

"The unfortunate events in Virginia suggest that defensive weapons are needed even more on college campuses than in the shopping malls and theatres and restaurants."

He was serious. And thus the quotation marks around his title.

One question immediately came to mind: does this man, this "professor," carry a firearm to class? Would he? Can such a person possibly be a worthy mentor to our children, much less to students of the law?

I've always believed the posturing of the National Rifle Association—Charlton Heston screaming at a podium that the Feds would only take his musket from his "cold and dead hands"—was a salacious joke. Even so, I excused the actor. Charlton may have seen *Ben Hur* once too often in his elder years. Maybe he didn't remember his part in *The Ten Commandments* as well.

But today comes a "Professor of Law," declaring that the population of the United States of America should arm itself against itself.

I am aghast.

Writing further seems a waste. Franks and his ilk will never believe that a civilised country can exist without a vast arsenal of killing weapons in every closet. And I myself must admit that after the Katrina barbarism [7] and its fallout—hordes of semi-humans walking the streets with many weapons, with few police and no conscience to restrain [8] them—I have considered the possibility of purchasing a gun myself.

I have not done so. Yet.

But when our universities start preaching the use of the physical instruments of death, rather than logic and aesthetics and moral values, I begin to wonder.

I begin to remember my Aunt Margie, as luminous and joyful a creature as ever walked the earth. I remember my cousin Mark, a great softspoken spirit, full of the happiness and innocence of youth.

I begin to wonder what it will take to simply live life without taking life.

Teach that, Professor Franks, and I will take the class.

URLS

[1] www.crimelibrary.com/notorious_murders/mass/whitman/index_1.html
[2] appl003.lsu.edu/artsci/frenchweb.nsf/$Content/Cajun+French+Definition?
OpenDocument
[3] www.ci.austin.tx.us/library/ahc/whithome.htm
[4] www.utexas.edu/tower/
[5] www.nola.com/news/t-p/letterstoeditor/index.ssf?/base/news-9/
1177049784184120.xml&coll=1
[6] www.vt.edu/
[7] www.hbo.com/docs/programs/whentheleveesbroke/
[8] www.opendemocracy.net/globalization-climate_change_debate/disarmed_3794.jsp

Undercurrent

A grizzly Vietnam vet, motorcycle hound and great survivor sends an electric miracle.

He'd phoned twice the week before, and I'd returned the call to his hotel voice mail on both occasions, but we hadn't connected. So when the 350-pound biker widely known across the deep south as "Grizzly" called me again last Thursday, I was as prepared as could be for another of his semi-annual communications.

He was back home in Baton Rouge.

"Shit fire, Jimbo, I called and called, where the hell were you?" he yelled without preface as I picked up the phone in my office.

"Out of town, Griz, but I got your messages and left a couple for you explaining where I was."

"Bro, my mind can barely handle punching in the eleven numbers it takes to get you from here in BR. No way am I gonna deal with some weird electron woman telling me to 'Press 22 to access your messages' and 'Press 87 to play your messages backwards in non-sequential alphabetic order derived from the various species of cloven-hooved beasts described in the Old Testament'. She ain't even real, and this woman's ordering me around. Don't say 'please' or nothin', so I ain't doin' it, and that's that. So no, I didn't get no messages. Just as well. I was getting a bit crazy. A lot crazy. That's the way my old head rolls when I start focusing too hard on just one thing nowadays."

"What was happening? Your marine convention again?"

"Yeah, that's it. They wanted to make me president. Then I decided I wanted to be president. Lost by three votes out of a couple thousand. Good damned thing I lost, too. Those sunsabitches would have made me actually *be* president. Me, I just wanted to be *elected* president. There's a difference."

"I know, Griz. There's lots of that going around right now."

Being there, coming home

Ed "Grizzly" Riley was an active member of The Legion, a large group of ex-United States marines, the majority of whom who have faced the extreme conditions of war and now communicated and banded together once a year as a nationwide support group. The now-civilian vets in the southeast also gather for a week once a year in New Orleans to drink beer and try and find order in the universe.

Griz—once an uneducated, extremely poor 17-year-old volunteer soldier known affectionately to the corps of *Semper Fidelis* as Buck Private Edward P Riley III—earned his place in that organisation the hard way. He hadn't much going for him when he joined up except his natural country-boy talent as a sharpshooter, but for the marines that was enough. They fed him three large meals a day, gave him free clean clothing, honed his marksman's eye in Basic and in advanced infantry training (AIT), and schooled him on the workings and maintenance of state-of-the-art, high-powered, long-range, single-shot rifles. They promoted him to private first class (PFC). Edward P was mighty happy.

Then suddenly, the honeymoon was over. Ten days after completing AIT, he found himself left dangling with a bag of dried and canned food in a hastily constructed blind seventy feet above a jungle floor in Cong-occupied South Vietnam. He had mimeographed orders in the pocket of his "gilly suit"—a self-assembled camouflage uniform of colored burlap—telling him to kill and then categorise anything he saw move below him, because there sure as hell weren't any "friendlies" in his assigned neck of the woods. There was a buddy marine hiding out somewhere down there, a combination of spotter and guard who was supposed to be the PFC's safety net. Somewhere down there.

They'd go out in groups of two to five for two days or ten, depending on the mission, and they'd trek way up into boonies infested with VC and NVA regulars, a pretty harrowing experience in itself. But mostly Edward P squatted in his elevated nests thinking about life. As ordered, every so often he took one—a life—at a distance of over a mile if he had his favorite 300 H&H Magnum, unsilenced. Taking off the silencer made for increased accuracy. "Further away, safer you were, especially with the noise that baby made," he'd told me the drunken night we first met, "that way the Slopes couldn't track back to you. Pretty scary, them walking all around down below, sometimes get caught with them camping right underneath if your spotter was a doped up and not watching. You just holds your water and don't eat or hardly breathe 'til they move on."

PFC Riley was sent out frequently to wait in trees for the better part of two years. Then he re-upped for another two. It was something he could do, and do well. He was proud to be a part of a truly elite force of over a thousand deadly marine sharpshooters, a group that was put together when the contract shooters being brought in from outside the services by "Project Phoenix" kept mysteriously disappearing with American weapons which, though not always legal, were certainly lethal.

Edward was good at his job. After the first year, he'd been promoted to corporal. Then, after making two quick kills on the same mission at 608 and 610 yards, using only an M-16—an astounding feat—he received a field promotion to E-5. Buck Sergeant Riley.

But at the end of his time in service he was retired as a corporal, because though the shooters were revered within the corps, things weren't quite the same on the outside. His superiors were under instructions not to publicise what his job had been, much less that he had done it well and under extreme conditions of duress and danger. Back in their Washington press mills, the Pentagon's community-affairs pundits considered the term "sniper" pejorative. In Second World War movies a "sniper" was stereotyped and cast as a despicable, heartless creature only The Enemy employed. The job description remained a negative PR label stateside, and such a cowardly non-person was considered not acceptable as a civilised tactical weapon. The "police action" was having a hard enough time as it was. 'Nam was slow at gaining any popular support in the late 1960s, even among the flag-wavers. The generals figured there was no sense telling the macho US public that the Good Guys used "snipers."

Naturally, when the corporal was returned to civilian life, he was completely out of contact with reality and dangerous as hell to boot. The only steady job he had had in his life was killing people, one at a time and from a distance. The government had trained him, and he had been good at his task. Now after over four years, they had decided that maybe he shouldn't do it any more. They told him to stop and to forget he had ever done it. They "rehabilitated" him and counselled him on temper control. They gave him free training on how to be a mechanic, and the shrinks offered him as many prescription drugs as he could ingest.

Corporal Edward P Riley III went Awol from what his doctors called reality, though the heavily-sedated soldier was eventually released from governmental care, and certified "no longer a risk to himself or the community." At his exit, the marine paymaster gave him $3,000 cash in separation and "total disability" bonuses, telling him he'd be receiving a like amount monthly for the rest of his life, or at least as long as he stayed crazy. The doctors had noted in his records that the two periods were likely to coincide.

MPs pushed the discharged and supposedly defused assassin out the gate of the army processing station where he'd been temporarily detailed for psychiatric evaluation in Fort Lewis, Washington, and told the young marine where the bus station was located in nearby Seattle. He could walk the dozen or so blocks in no longer than fifteen minutes, and there was a bus headed south in just half an hour.

The corporal was not to make the noon Greyhound. His route took him directly in front of Bob's Harley Shop. He looked in the window, and saw large motorcycles. In particular he spied a used metaflake black Duo-Glide priced at $2,200, walked in the door and plunked down twenty-two fresh $100 bills without a word. He counted out an additional $300 for two Harley t-shirts and a thick pair of upper and lower leathers, then walked into the shop's greasy bathroom, removed his marine class A uniform and left the cotton-and-wool remnant of his military experience in a wad next to a stack of pink urinal cakes. The six-foot-four baby-faced 21-year-old walked onto the bike showroom floor clad in brown-black cowskin. The owner stared and then commented, politely, "Hey man, you look like one of those big honkin' grizzly bears from up north."

So it was Grizzly who kicked the seventy-four cubic inches of cold steel engine to life. And it was Grizzly who took seven months riding the two-wheeled American icon home to Louisiana, hoping he'd find himself there.

When he arrived, he found his mom and dad had passed away a year or so earlier, and that he was the sole heir of a one-story two-bedroom brick house with a large garage in Baton Rouge, Louisiana. He hadn't received much mail in his tree.

He parked his bike and took his medication. It didn't help much.

The electric highway

Griz was calling me from the front room of that house now, thirty-one years later, to catch up on what had been happening in the few months since our last communication. We'd been riding buddies through most of my graduate school and teaching years in the early 1970s. The Flying Gonads Racing Club had somehow adopted me as a fellow Bad Boy, and Griz was the president of the Gonads. We bonded.

"I ain't ridin' no more, Jimbo. That beautiful big ole Hog is sittin' outside gatherin' dust and rust," he orated into the phone.

"This part of your born-again rules?" I asked. Griz had found Jesus a few years earlier when the local Veteran's Administration Hospital had upped his already-stratospheric medication levels with a new potent hormone-leveler.

"Naw, man, I'm kinda off that too, though I found there's something bigger. At least bigger than most of the religion marketing biz. Like a groove, you know, the sort of groove a real blues man finds in those middle of the night jams with nobody in the house but the band. Gettin' to that high place where it only matters to yourself, you know, and you're doin' it all by yourself, without any of that artificial bullshit."

"Without drugs, Griz?"

"That's it, man. No nuthin'. Though I'd be lying if I said I even remembered what that was like. At least until about a month ago. That's when it happened."

"You've got something important to tell me."

"Yep. I figure you're the one'll understand. Rest of the gang long gone, most of 'em dead, Weird Harold he don't even know what day it is most of the time. I couldn't tell the marines—well, I did, but it was just a biker story to them, nothing bigger."

"Lemme hear," I said, wedging the phone between my ear and shoulder, and preparing to continue my work while filtering most of the Griz narrative out. This had happened before, these long narratives made of valium and lithium and melaril and thorazine and whatever else the Veterans' Hospital had in a quantity sufficient to sedate a moderate-sized Tyrannosaurus Rex. I like the guy, though, and am normally willing to listen if it will help him sort through the pharmaceutical haze. Usually the tale was disjointed, unrevealing, and without surprise.

Not this time.

"Since the boys elected me president of the Leathernecks, I keep having to do these public-service things to show regular folks we bikers ain't all hoodlums and outlaws. I been mighty depressed this last year, and to try and get out of it I had let myself get into another of these damned Fearless Leader gigs. I was more messed up than usual, and gagging back half a dozen 'scripts twice a day. All I wanted to do was sleep, which helped, but the pillow was getting boring as hell."

"One of the things everybody thought I should do is ride in this "Toys for Toddlers" caravan. Couple thousand bikers get together over in

Cajun territory and ride 150 miles into New Orleans, and for every mile each biker rides, a sponsor donates a buck to this toy fund for needy kids. Even the damned Republican governor of this state rides. Lotta national PR involved here. Network news coverage and the like."

"So I get this call from the Pagans bike club up in New Jersey, saying they would sponsor me if I would ride one of their bikes, a seriously chromed and customised set of wheels with their club name painted all over it. They said they'd even ship it down on the train for free, just as long as it got seen by as many people as possible."

"Well, I couldn't refuse that, not and save any face at all, even though I wasn't really excited about riding someone else's colors, especially in a big crowd with a lot of rookies. So I said yes, and a few days later this big crate arrived. It held one of the most elaborately tooled Harleys I ever did see, and I've seen a lot of 'em. 'Pagans' in big script letters on both sides with little red horns on the 'P'."

"Comes the morning of the ride, I wake up before sunrise to travel the forty-five miles west to the rallying point in Lafayette, and before my ass is out of bed I know the day is bad news. Thunder is shaking the house like there's an artillery battalion stoked on crystal meth outside. Rounds dropping all over the place. Rain, lightning, bimbamBOOM here it comes, over and over. But I said I'd ride and I'm a man of my word. You know that, hunh, Jimbo?"

"Uh, yup, yes, sure, Griz, always," I mumbled, caught off-guard.

"So I put on my yellow plastic rain suit, duct tape all the seams tight over my boots and gloves, hop on that big mother of a bike, cut on the lights, and I head out through the rain."

"About half-way, in that elevated part of I-10 that crosses the Henderson Swamp, the storm really gets to cranking, the wind pushing even me and that heavy bike side to side and the lightning just exploding all around, reflecting up off the wet concrete and into my face. That's when it happened."

"One minute I'm sitting on this Harley, and the next I'm naked, sitting in a brightly lit room on a plastic chair that's sticking to my butt, looking around. I'm waiting for the bus, I know, but I don't know which bus, so I just wait. Out of the marines, waiting for that bus south. It all seemed so perfectly natural, like sure enough, I had planned to be there and this was the right thing to do."

"Then somebody said somethin' to me and zip I'm on my couch at home, sitting there nice and still-like. I can feel a smile on my face.

Feel it. Local news is on the box and the old lady is asking me if I want tea with dinner. I ask out loud where I been, and she comes into the room, looks at me, says 'Grizzly?' real scared-like. I says, 'What?' and she says 'You sure don't remember, do you? And now you're back'. Then she cries to beat all hell for the better part of half an hour before she tells me what she meant.

"The driver in the semi behind me saw the whole thing, saved me from getting killed, and I still don't know his name. Told the cops that the lightning bolt hit me dead on top of my head, and that the whole bike glowed right down to the ground, even though the lights blew out and glass was flying out behind me."

"Must have killed the engine right then, but I had a pretty good head of steam and the bike rolled about a mile before it came to a halt. Driver said I was letting off yellow smoke from my rain suit, black smoke from the bike engine and white from my beard, which was smoldering pretty good. Amazing sight, my trail. Made it easy for him to follow me. He told 'em I had control all the way, even put tried to put the kickstand down before I fell over. Didn't fall off, though. My gloves were fused onto the rubber handlebar grips and my boots onto the foot rests. My beard was filled with melted yellow rubber."

"I didn't remember my name, but they got my license, called the old lady to tell her that the paramedics had checked me out, and I didn't seem to have any physical damage, even if what they had been told was true about the lightning, which they couldn't prove. But more importantly they were disturbed that I was carrying lots of drugs, even though they were legal and in my name, and that I was completely disoriented."

"I love Wanda. She come pronto with a truck for me and the bike, and I was home barely two hours after the strike. She shipped the totaled bike back to New Jersey, and when it arrived the Pagans called her to say they hoped I was dead. She told them that not to fret, that for all practical purposes I was."

"I sat on the couch for a few weeks, and she said I seemed pretty happy, other than not knowing who I was or remembering anything for more than ten minutes."

"Then I woke up. I left the waiting room. And I took up right where I left off. Went to the Legion convention the next week like nothing ever happened. Got a little hyped and confused. Called you, but couldn't find you. Took a few valium and made it through the knot. Decided that being an officer in things is not really what I want to do. The marine years weren't exactly the most pleasant in my life, but it was the time that has most affected who I am and what I did afterwards."

"Until this happens."

"Now here I sit, bored as hell again, and starting to think about the future for maybe the first time in my whole damned life, but I don't feel so bad about what's happened, I'm only taking half my 'scripts at most, and I think I need to be doing something constructive. Getting back out there with people who do things, rather than just think about the past and sort it all out."

"So, I'm calling you again. S'way it is, bro. You need a bodyguard or a stagehand?"

"We're happening, Griz," I said without thinking. Then started thinking *Can I really stand the distraction?*

I told him I had a few gigs coming up where I could use a strong arm to change stage sets quickly. And of course I'd always liked having him around. He vowed he'd be here on a moment's notice.

I thought again about our linked pasts, felt a bit ashamed, and said: "Sure. Why not? I'll call you with the dates."

Before he hung up, Edward P Riley III said he'd travel the interstate on the bus this time around.

Cry Oncle!

The real New Orleans melts under the arc-lights of a TV commercial that seeks to fake its authenticity. There's sweat in the memory.

The golden sunlight of a summer afternoon warmly caressed the lush, verdant expanses of a typically southern, rural antebellum scene. Across the vast green lawn, family members strolled and excitedly exchanged reminiscences in French, as was their custom, in anticipation of the more formal gathering that was to come. The tableau was pure Seurat, women clad in pastel cottons and linens, men in tailored grey and black morning coats.

Uncle Ben approached his great nieces, a smile spreading broadly across his gentle mahogany face. The two handsome young girls stood waving in the hallway of his family's lavish plantation home. Jade, their mother, watched the old man's approach, knowing that *Mon Oncle*, as she had affectionately always called him, would once again come to her aid with his tantalizing sauces.

What had he in his bag? A jar of *Creole* sauce, or perhaps *Louisianne*, or a jar of *Nouvelle Orleans*? She knew that, with his help, she would feed her family and friends a grand meal, whatever he had brought.

Jade was right.

Later in the afternoon, a pianist played ragtime under the towering front veranda. The dutiful niece carried her steaming main dish between the stuccoed columns of the porch and out onto a linen-covered table set amidst the flourishing grass of her front yard, a huge space that sloped in the distance to the Mississippi River. Close to the house between the colonnades of ancient oaks, her hungry guests waited.

In her heart Jade thanked her Uncle for his *idees recettes*. His recipe ideas were always perfect for the occasion. Sensing her approval, the kindly man beamed in her direction, a familial affection apparent in his eyes. The rest of the family applauded. The pianist brought up another jaunty chorus of ragtime music. Happiness reigned.

On the plantation

"Cut. Cut! I can see the bloody rain pooling on the dinnerware! Kill the lights. None of this sounds or looks like the Old South. This is not one bit New Orleans! None of it!" yelled the ascotted British director.

Massive ten-kilowatt spots and multiple grids of nine-lights clicked and hummed as they switched off and faded into darkness. The actors and actresses, all English-speaking African-Americans except for The Parisian Niece, scurried to the warmth of the modern cafeteria kitchen, the soles of their shoes stained chartreuse by the dye used to make the winter lawn look like summer. Two stories of cleverly tinted blue-sky backdrop cloth fluttered on sandbagged thirty-foot iron masts as the freezing January shower again pelted the set. One of the lesser lights exploded, sending a fine, stinging cloud of glass pellets over 84-year-old Freddie Washington, Uncle Ben for the last two ad campaigns, and the slowest-moving of the actors. A New Orleans native, he put his teeth in his pocket to protect them as he continued on toward the break room. They'd been loose all day, and he thought he was coming down with a cold.

He didn't understand a word of the French that the woman from Paris had been saying in the commercial. She was intimidating to Freddie who, in his own neighbourhood, was used to being deferred to with a certain gentility and respect, even among the meanest of company.

"The woman a bitch," he thought as Jade bumped him aside while hurrying to the heated room, but he refused to say a word out loud. All he had to do to get paid was keep his teeth in his mouth during the takes and smile broadly.

The American actor playing the part of The Nephew, however, was complaining loudly, as he had between every set-up for the last three days.

"I mean, what the hell we doin' here, man?" he screamed at the top of his voice. No reaction. The crew had long since learned that ignoring him was safest. Any recognition and he got louder. Still he persisted.

"This plantation nothin' but nigger hell—the brothers didn't come here from the motherland wearing no cast-iron 'welcome home' bracelets— they wasn't on no fuckin' *vacation*, man. And then they get stuck here bein' *free*—meanin' they no longer slaves, but now they got *real* slave wages and maybe a shack, and now they got to *buy* they own food from the Man. So here we sit with this honkey muthahfuckah, and he got us actin' like we *own* the place? It's a sin, man. It's a fuckin' sin."

"A sin for which you get paid $225 dollars a day," yelled the location producer from somewhere off-set. "Unless I finally get too tired of hearing this spiel. May I remind you that yours is currently listed as a non-speaking part?"

The Nephew quieted immediately. He needed the wages he was to receive in cash when the shoot wrapped. He walked into the craft services tent. Bottom line was there were side benefits to the gig. This bit about being able to eat all day was a definite perk.

In the sequestered side-kitchen, Jade sat drinking *Provençal* wine with the advertising executives. The French agency had agreed with the British production company that American wines would likely be unpalatable, so an extra catering expense had been approved as a budget line item. Consequently, they'd hired an experienced sommelier in Paris who'd assembled and transported several cases filled with a variety of admirable vintages on the plane from DeGaulle airport.

From real to hyperreal

Jade, too, had been imported to play The Niece's part. She hated being so far from real civilisation. Even those who spoke French here, like the first assistant director, were not understandable.

"Quelques-uns de ce patois Acadien soi-disant," she speculated to the casting director. The language she had been hearing was supposedly some of this Cajun *patois*.

The agency had, unfortunately, decided that Jade's own French voice was far too French, and didn't sound like it should for it to be considered by Parisians as southern and American and antebellum. After all, this commercial would only air in Europe. The account executives were already auditioning females back at the hotel, looking for the proper accent. Something cruder was needed, they thought. Rougher. Something unrefined. Like America. Like New Orleans. Especially like New Orleans.

The food stylist had already dumped the last take's steaming entrée into the overflowing waste can, with her assistant preparing to strategically stuff a fourth platter full of the product with dry ice. The ice was a perfect tool for giving the food the steaming, appetising, just-off-the-stove look that made audiences salivate. She'd already soaked and dried another bowl of rice with glossy liquid glue so that it would both remain shiny white and stay in place as the sauce was ladled over it. "Savoury" had been the director's sole descriptive instruction, and she knew how to deliver savoury.

Dry ice and white glue.

Three make-up artists were back at work lightening the skin of each of the eight actors and actresses. The English director had decided that the actors and actresses he had chosen were, after all, too dark to be considered properly "Creole," and was determined to preserve his idea of authenticity. After all, hundreds of thousands of people would be persuaded to buy this product as nourishment for their families on the perceived truth of the advertisement.

Art and Commerce

As the American executive-in-charge-of-production, setting up all the monumental multi-cam thirty-five millimetre film logistics in pre-production, I'd helped spend a substantial amount of the approximately $4 million the thirty-second commercial would finally cost after post-production polishing was completed. There were massive thirty-foot cranes, dollies with straight and rounded tracks, electrical generators with hundreds of yards of cabling, gaff and grip trucks, and a hundred personnel to house and feed on location for the better part of a week.

I had taken the job willingly, fully knowing the ethics of the work. Never a rich man, but after many years at least modestly financially solvent, I had bought my first-ever house, a serious fixer-upper, and was in the midst of the overwhelming process of house restoration in New Orleans. I needed to maintain serious cash-flow. There were more toilets to be bought, dozens of walls of new sheetrock to be installed, floated and sanded. Wiring and plumbing to be laid. Taxes and insurance to be paid.

I could not afford to hold out for Art. I needed immediate and ongoing Commerce. Thus, in my own weak-willed way, did I help perpetuate another of modern civilisation's illusions, and delusions, about the heart of my-home-town.

On the other hand, the sauces were quite tasty.

A song for the kitchen, a song for the heart

When the Vegetable Man returns, can normality in New Orleans be far behind?

I heard him again, just moments ago.

He's been crisscrossing the neighbourhood all morning, his voice deep, strong and melodious: "Mirletons, I got ya mirletons," he sings, with feeling. "Apricots, nice sweet apricots, oh yeah got ya yellow squashes and ya turnip greens an' they some kinda sweet an' good ones today," he intones, the final "daayyyyy" drawn out as a long last note, echoing in diminished returns as it travels down Marigny street towards Royal.

The dilapidated loudspeaker on his even more decrepit truck crackles and whistles with the changes in the old man's voice. "Here I yam, an' I know ya lookin' fo' me, yes indeed I do. Got them fresh Georgia peaches."

The Vegetable Man is back. His moniker pronounced "Veh-jee table." 73 years of age he proudly announces, driving a smoking Chevrolet pickup truck that was already old when he bought it in 1981, he manoeuvres the potholed streets of New Orleans's Faubourg Marigny and Bywater with care. Atop his truck bed, a rusting tin roof is supported by splintered two-by-two-inch boards, which shake side-to-side rhythmically as he passes through the neighbourhoods calling out the lyrics of his edible opera. The metal sheets, salvaged from destroyed sheds in the ninth ward, extend out over the back and sides of the truck bed to protect dozens of boxes of pristine, tissue-packaged and beautifully-arranged cargo.

An urban 21st-century Mona Lisa, made of fruits and vegetables, framed in scrap metal.

The Vegetable Man is back. Back in New Orleans. Plying the streets of his old neighbourhood for the first time since 29 August 2005. He has been in exile since the storm and he now tells everyone he meets that Houston, Texas, is not a place for civilised human beings to dwell.

"Got no goddamned soul over there, them goddamned sidewalk cowboys," he says. "Cowboys. Them ain't cowboys. Wearin' boots was made in Taiwan, eatin' store-bought frozen hamburgers while they actin' fo' all the world like they wuz the one what killed the cow. *Ain't* no goddamned cowboys in Houston."

How I relish the sound of his voice, a curse-filled, grumpy, definitely un-PC rumble that my neighbours and I associate with normalcy and back-handed off-colour humour.

And we need him. Though there are two mom-and-pop grocery stores now open nearby, our neighbourhood supermarket is still in shambles. The nearest large food outlet remains half an hour away by car, if the traffic is right. Many people who live here are elderly or lower-income, or just don't have vehicles. Public transport is a nightmarish joke with, at best, one in ten bus routes functioning with anything near a regular schedule. So it takes an effort to get good food. Food The Vegetable Man now brings to us.

Though I made a mistake the other day, when he first showed up.

I was so happy to hear him back home that I ran out into the street to buy anything he had on hand. I filled a great bag with fruit, even though I myself had driven out to the suburbs to get groceries only the day before, and when he handed me my change—a mere fifty cents—I told him just to keep it.

But he reached out and stuck the coins back in my hand, the calluses of his palm scratching my fingers. "What you think," he told me, a smile creeping in under his grimace, "you thinkin' I one a' them *titty-bar* dancers? I look like I could dance aroun' a *pole* at my age? Don' need no goddamned *tips*, boy."

You have got to love The Man.

I ask him if he gets worried riding around with a wad of cash, entirely exposed to the Bad Guys. There are many of them, in spite of the New Orleans police department's efforts, still-flourishing groups of thugs who have taken to frequent muggings and armed robbery in this downtown corridor along the river.

"'Em boys ain't foolin' with no Vegetable Man," he proclaims, tugging mightily at his suspenders and scanning the street end to end with his chin held high, as if daring anyone to contradict his words. "I be layin' some *wood* on 'em they fool wit' me." He points to the side of his truck bed. A gnarled and chipped baseball bat lies amidst the stacked cantaloupes.

"All I ever needed, all I need now," he says. "Don' wanna kill 'em. Jus' wanna make 'em take pause an' think on they evil ways."

He seems so sure, so confident, that for the moments I stand there, I believe him. I believe in his positive worldview. I believe.

"Gotta make a livin' now," he tells me as he climbs into the dented driver's side door. "Stand here lolly-gaggin' all mornin' wit' you, I ain't gonna make me enough money to cover my gas."

He cranks the engine. Another great cloud of suffocating black and grey fumes explodes from the rear of the truck, rising from beneath the bed. I cough and cover my mouth.

He notices this in his rear-view mirror.

"Goddamned public service I'm doin'," he yells. "Killin' skeeters. An' I do it for free."

I hear a gravelly half-chuckle as he puts the truck in gear with his right hand, waves with his left, and ever-so-slowly drives off. It is then that I hear him say something over the roar of the engine and squeaking springs. His pronouncement is faint but unmistakable.

"Boy thinks I'm a goddamned *titty-bar* dancer."

I never would have thought that hearing that particular combination of words would make me feel so good.

"Got yer ripe tomaters, got yer veh-jee tables..."

The upper crust

A real-estate New Orleans courtship with the formidable Priscilla Fogarty is an experience to be savoured. Or survived. Or survived.

"Look at those balconies," said Priscilla Fogarty, short, shrill, and solid. Priscilla, brilliantly and unnaturally redheaded, was encased in a polished silver linen suit that looked as unwrinkled and shiny as medieval armour. Her name and corporate logo stood emblazoned on a twenty-four-carat gold shield that decoratively protected the severe up-slope of her left breast pocket. I had noticed over the weeks of our association that Priscilla's heavily-constrained body—like her manually-applied features—never changed shape or flexed, whether she was sprinting up stairs to point out a skylight or standing on tiptoes to disable a burglar alarm. There was no doubt that the woman's garments, above and below, were every bit as formidable as Priscilla herself.

If I was in the market for a home in New Orleans, she had decided, she would be the person to sell it to me.

Madame Fogarty had not stopped talking in my presence since our initial house-inspection appointment, two months earlier. She was recommended to me by a neighbour as "a bit much, but the only person to contact if you want to find the Real Stuff." Since at that point I knew of no one else, I acquiesced and called Priscilla.

She lived in an historic neighbourhood herself, so she had an interest in developing them properly, even if that meant occasionally letting in borderline artsy characters like me. The middle-aged supposed "TV person" who now stood beside her in jeans, high-top Converse All-Stars, and t-shirt.

"How sporty," she had remarked as I opened the passenger-side car door for our first house tour. She lifted her deeply tanned hand and exhibited it to me, palm forward, as the completion of her greeting. I leaned to inspect more closely, thinking that the required response. It was not. She would, in time, teach me how to react properly. She shook her head and lowered the hand back to the steering-wheel, as I climbed onto the oiled leather seats of her new Town Car convertible and closed the door. She scanned me up and down, twice, then put the luxury sedan into gear using only the tips of three manicured and ringed fingers.

"Our grandchild never dresses any other way, due, I am sure, to the degenerative influences of your MTV. Snoop Doggy Dog," she said knowledgeably, as punctuation, with a final, definitive motion of her nose toward my apparel. That particular Dog and I, she obviously felt, were in cahoots for the common degradation of mankind.

I was unprepared that first day. I received a vast amount of Fogarty information that was unrelated to housing. I was autobiographically overwhelmed.

Priscilla reveled in being an "active and attractive" 63, she told me in the third sentence of our acquaintance. She was quite well off and didn't need to work. But she needed to stay active. She had been a debutante, a member of the old-money Rex Court at Carnival, and her family had held membership at the Boston Club for three generations. This was her real hair colour, though no one believed it. She was indeed the real estate-agent who one way or another controlled all major home sales near the levee-side junction of St Charles and Carrollton Avenues. She had made the bend in the river her fortress. The rest of New Orleans was alright, if you didn't have to live there, and if you had someone to watch your car.

Her husband Edgar was a retired dentist who loved his terriers and his garden and painting watercolour landscapes and lived in the den with a television that was tuned twenty-four hours a day to the Weather Channel. He did not use the electronic device except as its contents pertained to his zinnias, elephant amaranths, and Russian mammoth sunflowers.

Be in no doubt

She did not like to cook or clean. She had a "coloured girl" who took care of those things for her, while she drove well-heeled people—I was something of an experiment—around to see houses that were on the market. She was able to look into other people's closets and bedrooms as a much-coveted side benefit. She wrote off her large American car each year as a legal and totally acceptable business deduction. It was essential to her livelihood, and she very seldom used it when she wasn't working, she said.

"I am always working," she added.

Lydia, her maid, arrived six days a week at 7am and left at 4:30pm. On Sundays, without this cook/housekeeper, Priscilla and the husband were obliged to fast through most of the day and eat only dinner. She could pour orange juice, but did not know how to work the electric coffee-maker or microwave, and at 63 did not care to learn. She and her husband consumed their one Sunday meal within the civilised confines of Arnaud's in the Quarter. She chose that particular *grande dame* restaurant, not because of the exquisite food, but because they had such trustworthy valet parking.

She hated the expense of that nondeductible Sunday dinner, anyway, and was not happy with Lydia's attitude, much less her need for a day off. The ungrateful woman was going to ask for a raise soon. Priscilla suspected it and was going to fire her housekeeper the moment the subject was broached. She had a replacement ready in the wings, had already interviewed her, an Oriental female. A grandmother. She felt an older woman would be more responsible. After all, she was a grandmother, too.

"Vietnamese. Grateful for the work, those people. Don't care about Sundays one fiddling bit. Heathens. Had a war in the jungle. Lost." Priscilla prided herself on her overview of contemporary world history as it pertained to her own life, though she didn't want to tip her hand to her current maid in case she was wrong. "But I never am, not about this sort of thing!"

Priscilla knew what would happen: "That woman will steal everything not nailed down in the time it takes a child molester to wink at a 10-year-old. That is, if she figures out in advance that I'm going to sack her."

Priscilla Fogarty had volunteered these facts before she released the automatic door locks at house-stop number one, less than a block down the street from where she had picked me up at my rented apartment. She did not open the car doors until she was good and ready. The two of us sat there—motor, radio, and air-conditioner running—for four-and-a-half of the first five minutes of our acquaintance, while the home-sellers peered at us anxiously through their drapes, wondering what the matter was, why we didn't come in.

I had expected that part—an embarrassing, furtive squirm through available properties, walking judgmentally through strangers' living rooms—and had braced myself for the prospect. But here was Ms Fogarty, a real-estate hurricane blowing out of a totally unexpected quarter. She would not go forward until she was ready. I would be paying her commission, but I was working for her, rather than the other way around, and I had best get used to the order of business. That was the message, right off the bat.

I was to listen to her monologue. So I listened. Patiently I listened.

The Fogarty family history was now well into its seventh week. I knew her son's name and age (Bruce, 45), his wife's (Bernadette, 39, "and she drinks"), the grandchild (little Tommy, 17, a 210-pound starting right tackle for Bonnabel High, "he's supposed to eat that much"). I knew that her husband was having troubles with the petunias on his deck. Slugs. And with his bowels. Cheese consumption. I knew how much her last two monthly utility bills had been. $379 and $401. The weather was extremely hot for her. Anything over 73 degrees Fahrenheit and 40% humidity was beyond human endurance, as were most aspects of New Orleans.

She also did not understand how any country could devalue its currency.

I had no reason to believe that she stopped talking when she left my presence, empty Lincoln or no. There was always the cellular. She randomly called twice an hour to make sure Lydia the hired help wasn't talking on her home phone, and even if there were no messages she always listened to her own announcement on the voice mail. Just to make sure no one had tampered with it.

This is what she's like

Priscilla was always famished by the time she had finished her Sunday afternoon rounds with clients, and would use her cellular phone to speed things up. She'd call home and have the husband waiting out front of their house to be picked up, then call the restaurant the moment she crossed Napoleon Avenue and tell the maitre d' she was on her way down St Charles, headed to the Quarter.

The maitre d' knew what to do. Arnaud's had not existed for over a hundred years on the corner of Bourbon and Iberville streets because it did not know how to cater to the locals' particular *regimes de cuisine*. Madame Fogarty always ordered the same thing each week. The restaurant's job was to insure that as soon as she walked through the cut-crystal door into the entrance hallway she would smell the deep, herbsaint-infused aroma of a piping hot Escargots en Casserole appetizer being laid on the crisp tablecloth of her favourite table. The baguettes would be steaming inside a cotton wrap, the butter fresh and lemony in a chilled silver tray, just as she liked.

She'd had the snails as a starter every Sunday for years, and could tell by scent if chef had the balance of flavors exactly right. She'd only sent it back once, carrying the dish in her own hands to the kitchen. Her husband had heard her raised voice, clear across the wide dining-room.

The dish had always been perfect since then, though it was rumoured that shortly after the incident, chef had purposely changed his day off to Sundays, forcing his *sous* to take on the burden of preparing Madame Fogarty's repast.

Someone had to carry the burden, for the greater good, but chef chose to delegate in this case, rather than serve. Thus avoiding any chance of unpleasantness.

As do many of us.

I myself took the chef's example to heart and did not buy a house from Priscilla Fogarty, even after suffering through our lengthy real-estate courtship.

I like to believe that in the end my decision was not avoidance, but rather a definite act of principle, such that I possess. On a more visceral level, as a New Orleanian, you might say that I had simply lost my appetite.

Lessons in the classics

A crawfish-loving angel of mercy in Manolo Blahnik stilettos lights up the night.

During my simultaneous house restoration and television-series production, I had been too busy to deal with the stove, what with alternating surprise bouts of plumbing and sound re-edits, and also the fits of depression that punctuated both processes. It was hard to cook, or at least cook interestingly, while living in a continuing, seemingly endless night-time purgatory of brutal, unending manual labor on the house, with only the prospect of waking to spend the daylight hours being artificially nice to people, acting the studio cheerleader as a producer must, coddling culinary divas—this was a cooking show. The work and stress loomed ahead day after day, a gruelling production schedule that stretched well into the next year.

Even on the weekends, the work was relentless. One particular Saturday my contractor had assigned me the job of knocking out ten feet of hundred-year-old cast-iron drainage pipe which had gone solidly blocked decades earlier and had now been bypassed by a new drain. The problem was the pipe had shifted so far with the new construction that the workmen couldn't put a wall back in place unless the thick six-inch-diameter pipe was removed.

The contractor had handed me a large sledgehammer and spoken the definitive words: "It's either you or a plumber and his assistant, them working at a total of $125 an hour. I'd say we're looking at four hours minimum here, rolling on weekend overtime."

I took the hammer.

It was not long before I realised that a twenty-pound sledge is not an instrument about which anyone will ever write poetry, even though I did remember myself as a child tapping my foot to the lyric "John Henry was a steel-driving man," and admired Mr Henry's finesse. I found that I was unable to even make a dent in the pipe, and now knew what a hero John Henry must have truly been. I was getting nowhere. My shoulders were aching and the sound of my blows upon the pipe were becoming progressively quieter. I knew I was losing effective strength, but I was determined to keep swinging.

An angel of mercy

At some point in my litany of curses—quickly reduced to four letters of verbalisation followed by an ever-so-mild *ping*! of contact between hammer and pipe—I heard someone downstairs knocking at my front door. I paused for a moment to make sure I had heard correctly. Yes, someone was knocking. I set the hammer head-down on the floor. As soon as I let go the handle, I knew I would not be able to pick it up again. My shoulders, arms, and upper body were already twitching with pain, after barely forty-five minutes' labour. I stumbled down the stairs to open the door.

"Whatever are you doing, child?" queried a lavishly arranged countenance set some six-feet-four-inches off the ground. "Have I arrived at an indiscreet moment? I do hope so."

The demure Ms Andromeda Summerville entered my home with a strut evocative enough to drive any number of gaunt fashion models from the runways of Paris to a lifetime of hawking foundation garments at WalMart. Ms Summerville, ever the star, was clad in designer sweats, tank-top and shorts, with a spotless set of $200 running-shoes on her dainty size-eleven feet. She had obviously been out for a jog, but sweat had not yet been added to the outfit.

"I'm hitting a pipe upstairs with a sledgehammer," I said.

"How terribly exciting for you. Shall we go see?" Andy swept up to the second floor to inspect the site of my demolition. "Where exactly have you been hitting this pipe?" she said, a small upturn at the corners of her mouth.

"I know. It's not working. I haven't made a mark on it, and the thing has got to go. I'll probably have to hire those same damned plumbers to come back and do more damage."

"Oh, sweet boy, let's not be hasty. Is this the device?" she said, lifting the twenty-pounder as easily as if it were a carpenter's hand-tool.

"That's the one."

"Now I'll be glad to give you a bit of assistance, but you mustn't let on to anyone. It would ruin the image that I work so hard to maintain."

"You're not going to hurt yourself, are you? That hammer can be dangerous."

"Darling, I've dealt with both the metaphor and the reality many times. Just stand back and let a girl do what she can."

Andy tapped the pipe lightly at intervals of a foot from the floor-joint to the ceiling, listening after each contact to the pitch of the noise. She came to a conclusion, stepped back a foot, and placed the hammer against the iron at a spot about three feet up. She took a deep breath. I could see the veins in the muscles of her biceps begin to swell. Then suddenly she drew back the sledge and loosed a swinging blow that ended with a deep crack, a rumble, and the collapse of the entire pipe above. I hadn't prepared for the circumstance of success, and the iron fragments hit my wood floor with force, gouging small holes in its waxed surface. But the pipe was down, and I would be resanding surfaces soon anyway. The damage was a small price to pay.

"Wonderful. Wonderful!" I yelled, patting the steel-driving Summerville solidly on the shoulder. "Andromeda, I adore you. And I am in your debt. You've saved me the horror of having to invite those monster plumbers back into my house, not to mention the expense. How can I ever thank you?"

"Dinner would be nice. I'm tired of eating alone, and I'm just not ready for the restaurant scene yet. A girl has to prepare for such things."

"Fine, I love to cook, and haven't had an opportunity or reason to really fire up the stove since I've moved in. Dinner, tomorrow night, seven?"

"I'll dress."

"I knew you would."

A crawfish for the queen

A hot bath in what is your own home will do wonders for culinary morale.

I didn't want to stretch too far the first time out, not until I got the hang of the eccentricities of this particular stove. And there lay another in this series of firsts: this was the first stove I had ever owned rather than rented. I decided to make something that I knew well enough to knock together on autopilot. I would make crawfish bisque, a dish any hungry person in south Louisiana is trained to make as soon as he or she can stand upright over flames. Crawfish, around my parents' house, were the plentiful free food that appeared in all the bayous and ponds every March. We caught them for the fun of it, and brought home bushel-baskets full of squirming crawdads with their claws poised to grab the thoughtless human. Might as well know how to cook the things. I did.

Ever the thoughtful guest, Andy called to confirm in mid-afternoon, and when she found out that I was already cooking, asked to come over early and watch the process, so she could witness the Way of the Kitchen.

"I'm going to settle down one day, and I want to be able to raise passion in every room of the house, including the kitchen," said my Texas-sized guest. She arrived in a provocative scarlet two-piece ensemble topped with some rather modernist accessories which she had arranged over a small lacy apron.

Did I fail to mention that Andromeda Summerville is a drag queen?

"I've got the outfit already, you see, to make hubby happy when he comes home. Now, if I could just concoct something edible that I didn't have to sneak in from an Oriental delivery service. Tell me everything, dear boy."

"We are going to make crawfish bisque, stuffing the heads."

"Oh, do, baby, yes. Make me obey your will."

"To the background lecture, then. You can help me chop ingredients while I talk." I handed her a knife and cleaned another place on the counter. The two of us began reducing vegetables into small sauté-able cubes as I gave my spiel.

"It is important to know the tradition of these dishes. The story makes the food even better for those who will eat it.

"Since we are in the Springtime height of the crawfish season, and since the wild crawfish are coming in so plentifully out of the Atchafalaya basin, we are going to take the time to make a traditional dish from the swamplands.

"It does fill an hour or two, if you're able to get fresh crawfish, because you must boil them and peel the tails, rather than simply buying them pre-cooked, peeled, and frozen into tidy blocks. But the cooking period is one of the reasons why the men like it so much—it takes them at least a six-pack of waiting around to eat."

"I have seen those same beverage-measured culinary methods used in my own native Texas. But solely in the incineration of large hooved mammals," said the delightfully-accoutered sous chef. "I hope you don't mind, but I'm taking notes," said Andy, and she was. There was a large pink poodle on the notebook she had removed from her handbag. The dog looked somewhat disgruntled, I am sure due to the fact that he had been forced to pose in the arms of a teenaged girl who signed her name "Love, Annette." A substantial rocket-nosed brassiere and rounded mouse-ear chapeau made all further identification unnecessary: Miss Annette Funicello had been the start of many a baby-boomer's sexual fantasies from 1955-58 on Disney's TV hit *The Mickey Mouse Club*.

Andy was scribbling madly. "If this doesn't get me the right man, I don't know what will," she muttered to Annette.

"There are at least forty-eight heads in a standard bisque," I started. "But you must remember that it is meant to feed six hungry people. Or just you and me, especially after we've talked about nothing but food for the better part of an hour preparing it, and have at least another hour beyond that to wait until it's done. But of course, we'll have to share with my three demanding cats, who have somehow developed a predilection for seafood with tangy sauces."

"Forty-eight? Heads? Two hours?" Andy's pen had stopped in its heavily looped tracks. "This cooking business takes longer than childbirth. At least my own, which was rapid. Seems Mater was anxious to get shed of me from the very start."

"It doesn't have to take that long," I said, ignoring the natal digression, "but some dishes are meant as much for the camaraderie that is enjoyed during the cooking as they are for the final goal, eating a meal together."

"Maybe I'll just do the easy thing and hire a chef. Someone colourful. A saucier. I've always loved the term saucier, haven't you?" said Ms Summerville, turning another page on Annette and her attendant canine. "But until then, I have you to give me lessons. I can pay my way if you've more pipes that need mending."

"My pleasure, even without the plumber's wrench. You can do this, Andy."

"Yes. If Tammy Wynette can cook, so can I."

And so she could. After we ate later that night, the gravy-spattered demoiselle happily took three containers of bisque back to her rented double shotgun home to feed the other tenants with the first products of her efforts as chef. She received raves, and was so excited at the prospect of more domestic stove-front action that the very next day she bought herself a fourteen-inch chef's toque. The tall white cylindrical hat brought her total height, counting the five-inch Manolo Blahnik spike-heels, to seven-feet-eleven-inches.

In the kitchen, like everywhere else, Andromeda Summerville would be noticed.

In one of our last conversations, she called from the hospice where she had moved a month earlier, to inform me of her decision to be cremated in a daringly low-cut Anne Klein sheath, fashioned of polished black silk, and complemented by two strands of her grandmother's pearls.

"Who knows who'll be waiting there," she'd said. "Dear boy, wardrobe for the afterlife is such a difficult decision, but you can't go wrong with the classics."

Indeed, Andy. You truly can't.

Epilogue

I understand that descriptions of alternative lifestyles may frequently not seem reality-based, and that I personally have presented (and will continue to present) a succession of these, here in the pages of **open-Democracy**. And so, I offer a 2006 news article [1], proving, I do believe, that warm-hearted Andromeda may actually be seen as quite normal, at least in New Orleans.

URLS

[1] www.neworleanscitybusiness.com/uptotheminute.cfm?recid=4912

Native to America

A Choctaw outrider, soul of his biker tribe, a man of many lives and names—it can only be Charlie.

I was eating my second raw dozen, balancing a paper plate full of food while standing on the slippery banks of the Amite River, a man dedicated to the consumption of honoree bivalves at the Oyster Festival in Amite, Louisiana.

Then suddenly I heard my name called out loudly somewhere behind me. I turned to see an oil-covered, snaggletoothed, long-haired biker in full leathers racing toward me with his penis in his hand.

The crowd parted instantly, jumping back and yelling as if a rabid dog had been dropped into their midst. Fathers put their hands over the eyes of children. Mothers stood agape and transfixed. A gaggle of teenaged girls tracked the movement of the tumescent organ across the fairgrounds with a synchronised formation of half-a-dozen pointed index fingers and a moist cloud of snickers and giggles. I ignored the gasp from my own female companion. She also had reacted quickly and now cowered behind me holding onto my shirt as if she was afraid of falling into the yawning gateway of the erotic maelstrom that had suddenly opened in the middle of a family-oriented food fair. My opinion of her diminished. I would have actually thought her better prepared for such an eventuality. I know I was.

Prepared.

Because Crazy Charlie had always known how to make a good entrance.

A Choctaw's change

"Get a look at this," yelled Charlie as he approached. He had a big smile on his face, which looked even crazier than I remembered, what with the loss of the majority of his teeth and the fact that his right eye now looked permanently forty-five degrees out to starboard. All options were always wide open for Charlie, who had never taken environmental or social setting into consideration when it came to the way he lived his life. He did what he was supposed to do, no matter where he was doing it. That was the way he operated. Now he was acting for all the world like it had been just yesterday we had last seen each other instead of the almost three decades that had actually passed. He seemed entirely unaware that displaying his sexual organ at a public gathering might somehow be deemed inappropriate by anyone.

"Charlie," I said. "I remember what it looks like." A full-blooded Choctaw Indian, he had been legendary among the university art school and biker bar crowds alike for the size of his Native American member, and had on more than one festive occasion such as this taken to "airing the peace pipe," which he would announce in his deep resonant voice as if it were an ancient tribal ritual. Thus my lack of surprise.

"Nope, you ain't seen it like this," he said to me now, still hefting the fleshy tube. "Just happened little over a month ago. Not used to it yet. It's shorter. I blowed almost four inches off, but I still got the biggest dick in the deep south. And now I got the ugliest one, too."

I couldn't help myself. I looked. I had to, or he would have stood there displaying himself for hours. Sure enough, the thing protruding from his pants was still of overwhelming proportions, and the end of it was scarred and twisted, looking rather like the bad side of the *Phantom of the Opera*'s face.

"Sure enough, it is still big and it's uglier than ever, but I think you'd better put it back up before we both get busted," I said.

"What?" Charlie looked around, and for the first time became aware of the crowd he had drawn. "Oh." He hefted his burden back into his pants and buttoned up his fly. "You'd think these folks never saw one before," he said, staring down one particularly angry-looking elderly woman who was standing less than a yard away.

"Bring back some memories, ma'am?" he asked directly to her face.

"Well, I never!" she said, spinning about and walking off quickly.

"That does seem more likely," mused he.

"Charlie, I'd like to introduce my friend," I said, reaching around with my left hand and dragging the poor woman forward. "Louise, this is Crazy Charlie. Charles, this gracious and charming person is Louise. I am quite sure she's never met anyone quite like you."

"No one ever has," he said, matter-of-fact. He smiled that wicked cracked smile again, and taking her hand gently in his, he bent over and gave it a delicate touch of his lips. "*Enchantez, mam-selle*," he whispered, looking up into her face with his soulful brown eyes. Charlie reserved his cultured side solely for the ladies. He was by no means an unintelligent man and could talk the talk, when he wanted to. "I promise that I am not as crude as I might seem, and I have always appreciated the sight and presence of a beautiful woman. You, my lovely Louise, are among the first rank of those." He bent and kissed her hand again, leaving a faint trace of 10W30 lubrication there, and then smoothly unfolded into his full six-foot-five height. Louise had not yet spoken, but was now staring at Charlie with something less than abject terror.

I broke the spell. "So how did you manage to 'blow off' a portion of your anatomy?" I asked politely.

Charlie was ready to tell his tale. He had always been one of the best around a campfire or a keg of beer when we both rode with the baddest band of hogs in the south, the Flying Gonads Racing Club. I still have the club shirt, which features a pair of Harley-Davidson wings flapping atop a wrinkled scrotum. Charlie was among the club's reigning elite, along with the moderately psychotic Weird Harold and the 350-pound ex-marine-sniper Grizzly, who had also recently reappeared in my life.

But that's another tale. This, this is about Charlie, because, in spite of the above narration, Crazy Charlie does not exist.

An Ootameewa bond

It was not from lack of trying. But at the time of Charlie's birth, in those low-water pre-casino days, the Indian tribes of south Louisiana were all but invisible. Few if any had a physical reservation, and though some tribes had legally incorporated to try and work as a unit to wrest their rights from the Federal government, the majority were vastly underemployed, if employed at all. Houmas, Choctaw and Chittimacha children in remote bayou country were offered little or no educational assistance, and the government seemingly felt even less motivation to seek out and better the lives of America's original repressed majority.

Half a millennium after Europeans appropriated their lands, dismissed their ancient social structures, and crippled their humanity with guns and alcohol, Charlie's parents refused to give their son to the invaders. His nativity went purposely unnoticed and unregistered, except with the tribal medicine man who had assisted in the birth and was awarded two live chickens and a small pouch of loose tobacco for his efforts.

In the course of his life, Charlie did not ask for, nor did he receive, a social-security number, a military-draft registration number, or a driver's license number. He paid no taxes and received no benefits. He had many names and lived many lives with an overriding glee, beholden to no one and nothing except his own strict moral sense.

For he was, after all, deeply righteous. And while bikers loved Griz, they feared Charlie, as they might fear their own shortcomings. Grizzly was the heart, but Charlie was the soul of this band of self-sustaining ruffians. They were their own government, their own tribe, and seldom strayed from their adopted neighborhoods.

Except for a single trip to the thirtieth annual biker rally in Sturgis, South Dakota, in 1977. When seven Gonads rode north into the company of tens of thousands of Harley owners.

Charlie hadn't cared for that. "Too many insurance salesmen wearing leathers. Weekend bikers. They got herds a' dermatologists pullin' their over-chromed scooters on trailers behind Porsches 'stead of ridin' 'em in. Too many seriously white men. First they steal our ponys, and now they steal our bikes."

Charlie was initially drawn to two-wheeled conveyances when he discovered as a child that one of the first widely-available and successfully-marketed bikes in America was call the "Indian." They were grand, loud, roaring devices. My own father owned one. But since that brand had long-since departed by the time Charlie rolled into enough cash and booty to trade for ownership, he took up Harleys as his own and never looked back.

"Scooters are a way of life, not just a way around," he'd declared to me when we first met. And he meant it.

With a vintage Triumph motorcycle and a university teaching job, I was something of a ringer mascot to the true outlaws, but was brought in as a full member after a long fully-bourboned night of my own barroom storytelling. And because my superficial respectability proved useful in getting the other members out of jams, legal, amorous, and otherwise. I liked almost every one of the two dozen members, bad or no, and their respect meant a lot to me, romanticised or no.

In what later proved to be a pivotal event, I had thirty years earlier managed to spring Charlie himself from jail at 3 am on a new-year's day, even though his one allowed call for assistance had caught me in the worst possible shape. I remember that the phone was ringing as I opened the door, stumbling into my living room on the return from a riotous party. I was admittedly drunk, stoned, hallucinating wildly (in those innocent psychedelic days LSD was deemed a recreational form of social rebellion), and possessed of only my Trumpet—as a Triumph was derisively though acceptingly dubbed by the Harley folk, because of their muffled sound—as a means of transportation.

"Jimmyboy, glad I caught you," said a familiar voice. "This is George Gunner. You remember me?"

I listened. The voice was swimming through my disoriented memory seeking a face that when found did not have the label "George Gunner." I knew I knew this person. I did not know a George Gunner.

"I fixed your carburetors a few weeks back."

Crazy Charlie. Sure.

"Where are you, Charlie, and why are you calling yourself George?"

"Easy, man, easy. I'm down here at the central lockup. They busted me on a DWI, drunk as a skunk, and they identified me from my wallet. I don't know how long that'll hold." Charlie had handfuls of arrest warrants out on him, for everything from firearms violations to possession charges. He also had carried a dozen different identities in the first year that I had known him. "I need someone to fetch me and quick," he continued. "I got bail money. I just gotta be released into the custody of someone sober. They won't even take your name. Can you come?"

"Charlie, I'm totaled myself. I'm illegal as hell. I just congratulated myself on making my way home walking six blocks from a party, and you want me to get on my bike, drive five miles of freeway, and dance right into a cop station?"

"I need you, man. You're the only one that can pull this off."

The pause was minimal. "Be there in half an hour," I said without conviction.

It took me ten minutes to get on my warmest rain suit, keeping to normal clothes instead of the leathers I would normally wear on such a frigid night, hoping that I wouldn't give the police one more clue as to my true nature and current condition.

I had done my best imitation of a sober and straight citizen, and had sprung Charlie without a hitch. Actually, riding my bike at the speed limit in the freezing cold on an interstate highway full of other inebriated new-year partyers had shocked me into a fairly admirable state of near-sobriety. I took Charlie another fourteen miles home to his bandito lair out in a bend of the Amite river, at the very end of a dirt path that went by the local name of Ootameewa. 1 don't know the exact origins of that name, but figure it has roots with Charlie's people. It is on no map, was and I suspect remains wilderness, and The Man gladly chose to ignore its existence.

Charlie had no shirt and no shoes, but hadn't even shivered when he dismounted from the back of my bike. He nodded his head as I left him. He owed me a big one, the nod said.

A Devil Boys encounter

From that day forward, he was my protector. No one, no one could mess with Crazy Charlie's bro. Word got around quickly that the mad biker had put me under his wing. It was absolutely bizarre. Even the faculty at school treated me differently. I was intimidated myself by the power Charlie's spectre seemed to possess in such different corners of the community, and how after another two years, his gift was undiminished. I was finally relieved when I was offered a job back in New Orleans, away from the Gonads' territory.

Charlie had never owned a phone. He said he liked to see faces and ears when he talked. His shanty had no actual address. He seldom even scribbled his signature, much less a letter, and like I said, he didn't like to travel outside what he considered his tribal grounds. I'd heard from friends about three years after I left that his troubles with the authorities had gotten worse, and that he had gone even further underground.

The Flying Gonads had disbanded. Weird Harold was killed in a car wreck. Grizzly had been born-again and was preaching at Veteran's Hospitals. Charlie was still there somewhere, they all said, somewhere well away from the Ootameewa, living below the surface of visibility to The Man.

Thirty years passed.

Now I had accidentally come back onto the fringes of his territory, and Charlie again stood in front of me, arm on my shoulder, acting like he hadn't a worry in the world.

"I blew off my pecker defending my dog," he started. He turned back to Louise, with a gracious look. "This might be unsettling and a bit lurid to a lady, Miss Louise, but I assure you it is true. If you'd rather not hear, I can understand."

"No, no, Charlie," she stammered. "I want to hear about your, uh, pecker." I took back my former lowered estimations of Louise.

He made a courtly gesture with a sweep of his arm and a bow to her, and proceeded. "I was standing in the parking lot outside Joe's East Texas Barbecue in Baton Rouge, you know, in that bad neighborhood off Dalrymple, me and my new pup, BeeBee, a Doberman. Just as good a dog as you could want, except a tad too friendly for my taste. I was actually hoping for something meaner. But he was a handsome mutt, and he liked me, and housebroke the day I got him, so what the hell, I figured.

"Me and the gents was having a few beers—like I said, this was just maybe six weeks ago at most—and we knew that we was putting ourselves in a rough place, what with going into the Devil Boys territory and all, but we wanted some of those damned ribs, and it's the only place you can get em. Everybody was packing, and me, I had that old double-barreled shotgun I sawed off back when you was running with the 'Nads, Jimmy."

I remembered the weapon well. Hard to forget such an evil-looking device. A blue-steel twelve-gauge, cut to less than two feet including stock and usually loaded with salt-shot, since Charlie in spite of his posing had never wanted to actually kill anybody. Though he'd do it when it was necessary, he had often told me, just to keep everybody honest. And he'd do it for me, if I needed it done. I had assured him that I did not anticipate such a necessity. Two hair- triggers, break-open action, no safety, and a recoil kick that I'd once seen crack a creosote fence post where Charlie had braced the gun's butt.

"I had my piece tucked inside my pants, cocked, loaded, and ready to go," Charlie explained, "because the Devils don't give you no warning on their home turf. They're just there, and they'll do you, and they're gone. Steal your car, grab your woman, shoot your ass, don't matter to them. And that's just what happened. This young guy zooms up on an old mid-fifties Duo-Glide panhead, don't even stop, grabs my pup, and is blowing up gravel trying to get out of there before we can blink an eye.

"So, me, I yell, then reach down and grab the shotgun to let the bastard have it, but the hammers get caught on my belt as I pull. I already got my finger on the triggers, and when I jerk to get the gun free first one, then the other barrel pops. Incredible noise. Blast took off the whole front of my pants along with the top third of my dick. Scared the guy on the bike so bad he dropped my dog and hauled ass."

"I didn't feel anything at all the first minute, then the salt started setting in and I thought I was going to die with the burning. The owner had already called the cops, and he came outside carrying his own pistol, but everything was over and it was just me standing there, empty shotgun hanging on my belt and no front to my pants. All the boys I was with had hauled ass because they knew some shit was gonna to come down, and the law was on its way. Couldn't blame them. When I told Joe the barbecue man what had happened, he brought out a garden hose and helped me wash the salt and blood off."

"I had to stand there squeezing it for the twenty minutes it took for the ambulance to come, or I'd of bled to death. BeeBee had run into the kitchen and hid under a table. Joe wouldn't let me inside though. He was afraid of being too nice to me. He's gotta live with them Devil Boys, day in day out. So there I was out in the gravel lot, a longneck beer in one hand and my bleeding pecker in the other, and I didn't even get to eat my barbecue. Pitiful."

Louise and I nodded. "Pitiful," we agreed.

"But it all worked out fine, 'cause even if I don't got the size anymore, the ladies seem to like it because it's got that twisted scar on top. One of a kind."

"I wouldn't have expected anything else, Charlie."

"Oops, shit, here comes a cop. If you need me, I'm around and I'll know. I still owe you, bro."

And, just that quickly, without another word or handshake or exchange of connections, he disappeared from my life again. My bro Crazy Charlie. Gone back to ground. Gone.

A man vs The Man

Been a while now, since that last encounter.

I figure if it wasn't me writing, and if Charlie was indeed still alive, he might actually shoot the person who had made him as visible as I just have, but probably seeing it's me he would just shrug, accept the burden of being made legendary, and let me live. This time.

Though whatever remaining spiritual debt he owes me would be washed away by his generosity.

I can just hear him saying: "You're on your own now, bro."

Crazy Charlie, a true Native to America, has always been on his own.

And I would take his company and friendship in a heartbeat to any offered by a nominal American government whose minions continue to exhibit less moral sense, fewer human values, and less loyalty to those they supposedly serve, than my friend.

Show 'em your peace pipe, Charlie.

The recurring anniversary of wilderness

Two years after hurricane Katrina there's blood on the streets,
blather in the politicos' mouths, fear in the residents' hearts.
Here is life on the edge in a beloved city whose roots are torn.

The date has come round again, and in search of a fresh feelgood head-line, national statisticians are reporting vast numbers in the news, in-dicating hugely increased percentages of returned population for New Orleans. They do this from afar, reading computer readouts compiled by other distant creators of factoids.

Those of us who live here can tell you the reported numbers are for the most part untrue. This is verified in a front-page article in the *New York Times* [1] ("Patchwork City: One Billion Dollars Later, A City Still at Risk," 17 August 2007; also here [2]), which has a graph showing two-thirds of the city still 50%-90% below its pre-Katrina pop-ulation [3].

That documentation is welcome, because the cunningly inflated statis-tics from previous sources provided false hope for not only locals but also for those living outside New Orleans, for people living in the Real World. For people, that is, who want us off their backs, their minds, their cumulative consciousness.

People who thought that if New Orleans's population was coming back [4], things must be OK.

But the former population of the Crescent City is not coming back, not in anywhere near the positive growth figures flaunted by White House spokespersons. Figures are manipulable, and population is fluid. That is apparent on even the most superficial examination of the George W Bush [5] administration's assessments.

And things are not OK.

An insecure city

The west bank of the city, largely undamaged by Katrina [6], is indeed recovering remarkably well, and that area is the basis of many of the population-increase figures, though the majority of people who lived in New Orleans prior to the storm did not live there. They lived on the east bank, the portion more widely known to and visited by tourists.

Today the east bank is barely here. Sure, the French Quarter and much of the central business district and Garden District [7] remain, but outside of a few brave enclaves of homes in isolated neighbourhoods, New Orleans is now basically the same sixteen-to-twenty-block-wide string of homes that followed the course of the Mississippi River in 1851.

Many, many fewer people. And yet that same east bank is the centre of the city's resurgence in crime.

The FBI released figures this past month which indicate that in 2006 New Orleans was the deadliest [8] place in America, had more murders per 100,000 people than even the worst urban areas. Realise, that assessment was concocted with the statisticians inflating our population enough to say that we actually had multiples of 100,000 people living here.

In 2007, the homicide rate already runs well ahead of that in 2006. It seems likely that New Orleans this year will once again be named [9] the "murder capital of America."

We do not relish this distinction.

The bloodbath continues in spite of the governor calling in a squadron of national-guard helicopters equipped with night-vision goggles and heat sensors to hover over the city, seeking out and tracking the Bad Guys. The army is still in our streets, their Humvees filled with automatic weapons. An almost completely-restored police department roams crime hotspots in donated cars. State police officers walk the tourist areas in groups of two or three. And now choppers hover over our homes in the darkness.

We are also armed with the ever-capacious mouth of our mayor, and with the seemingly limitless capacity for indecision [10], and bad decision, embodied by our local, state, and federal governments.

They seem to want us out of here, want us to go away. Since we threw out New Orleans's bloated system of seven separate assessors this past spring, the lame-duck bureaucrats have had their vengeance, with home assessments and taxation skyrocketing [11]. Taxes on my own homestead-exempted house went from an average of $79 for the past twelve years to almost $4,000 for next year. Hurricane "insurance" is now an exponentially rising item on both water and electric bills. Homeowner's insurance, even in protected and undamaged areas, has doubled and trebled.

While the real people continue their exodus, there remains a never-ending line [12] of politicians self-destructing, bloodying each other in their greed and arrogance, falling over each other in their eagerness to pick another dime from the corpse. In the weeks before the Katrina anniversary, yet another city-council member was led to jail for bribery [13] and embezzlement.

And the other, armed, Bad Guys, undaunted, keep killing each other, and us, the foolhardy souls who continue living in the midst of gun-studded, bloody wilderness.

The edge of life

Wilderness. The Bayou Sauvage wilderness area [14], an anomaly since it is actually located within the city limits of a major metropolitan area, New Orleans, now fits a larger definition of that word. In 2007 it shares characteristics with the more traditionally urban mortar-and-stone structure of uptown and downtown New Orleans, as they spread from beyond the immediate environs of the river.

That is to say, Bayou Sauvage is barely functional as a living habitat for anyone or anything.

Prior to Katrina, Sauvage existed as a federal park, beautiful though fragile wetlands and swamps, barely above sea level, curled on the brackish southern periphery of Lake Pontchartrain [15]. It swarmed with fish and gators, waterfowl, egrets, ibises and heron, and large predatory birds, including bald-headed eagles. It flowered in the spring and its short dunes held back the storms in the fall. Manatees had in past years made their way into its shallow protected waters.

My brothers and I boated and fished Bayou Sauvage [16] on many occasions, taking joy in the completely untamed nature of the place. It was magnificent.

Was.

Until the Big One brought much of it to water level, poisoned the trees with salt and pollution, and destroyed nesting grounds and food sources. Though we continue to hope for its rebirth, and we try to coax life back into its perimeters.

Generous, big-hearted volunteers from across America are taking part in replanting, building up undergrowth to hold the dunes and earth in place. Most of the city's residents donated their 2006 Christmas trees to the wetlands efforts. The trees were bundled and sunk at the swamp's edge, so silt and sand buildup would again form over the years as a protective barrier to storm surge. But the key words here are "over the years."

For now and the immediate future, the Wilderness Area sadly, but more rightly, bears the name.

The roots are torn

Meanwhile, also within the city limits, 70% of the city's overall tree canopy was damaged or destroyed in the storm. City Park, second in size only to New York's Central Park, took much of the brunt, with many of the massive live oaks' and river oaks' root systems submerged in salty lake water for over two weeks.

The long corridor of oaks leading up to the New Orleans Museum of Art [17], a green canopy of dozens upon dozens of century-old trees, all died in the winds and immersion. Every tree is gone. The removal of the dead trunks and branches finally accomplished, workers began bringing in living replacements this summer. But oaks grow slowly, and they will not regain their past stature in my lifetime.

Elsewhere, the trees on St Charles Avenue became entangled in the streetcar lines and were brutalised by the flying steel poles and cables that powered the cars. When the army [18] first entered the city, its mandate was to clear the streets. And so the soldiers did, though not gently. Hundreds of tons of limbs were removed and trucked to landfills. Even though the trunks of most of its tattered trees still stand, that landmark avenue is no longer the sculpturally-perfect shaded venue it was. The poles and electrical lines are being repaired at this very moment, but the trees themselves must do their own work, rebuild their own limbs and greenery.

Again, I will not live to see it restored to its former grandeur.

Even after two years of day-to-day living, it is quite hard to accept all this. The damage to both social and physical environments [19] remains, even seems to expand.

I am grudgingly ageing, and while time is passing quickly, I have less than no faith in government and its machinations to help speed recovery here.

Consequently, today I am forced to realise that, in spite of good intentions and massive good faith on the part of so many loving and concerned individuals, I personally may never see New Orleans emerge again.

From the wilderness.

URLS

[1]   select.nytimes.com/gst/abstract.html?res=F10B12FE3A5A0C748DDDA10894DF404482
[2]   www.spiegel.de/international/0,1518,500425,00.html
[3]   www.gnocdc.org/prekatrinasite.html
[4]   www.gnocdc.org/
[5]   www.boston.com/news/nation/articles/2007/08/25/bush_to_mark_katrina_
      anniversary/
[6]   news.bbc.co.uk/1/shared/spl/hi/americas/05/katrina/html/default.stm
[7]   www.bigeasy.com/maps/garden-district.html
[8]   blog.nola.com/murders2007/
[9]   abcnews.go.com/Politics/story?id=3299487&page=1
[10] www.boston.com/news/globe/editorial_opinion/oped/articles/2007/08/24/big_
      easys_difficult_recovery/
[11] www.npr.org/templates/story/story.php?storyId=12418084
[12] www.voanews.com/specialenglish/2007-08-26-voa2.cfm
[13] blog.nola.com/times-picayune/2007/08/councilman_oliver_thomas_plead.html
[14] www.recreation.gov/recAreaDetails.do?contractCode=NRSO&recAreaId=1291&
      agencyCode=127
[15] encarta.msn.com/map_701513994/Pontchartrain_Lake.html
[16] www.fws.gov/bayousauvage/
[17] noma.org/
[18] jurist.law.pitt.edu/paperchase/2007/08/army-corps-of-engineers-claims-
      immunity.php
[19] blog.nola.com/twoyearslater/2007/08/architectural_soul_of_the_city.html

Number One with a bullet

B-Stupid, MySpace, and an everyday tale of crime in the city.

To begin with, three episodes in an unfolding story:

United States House of Representatives—Subcommittee on Crime, Terrorism and Homeland Security of the Committee on the Judiciary (16 April 2007):

Katrina Impact on Crime and the Criminal Justice System in New Orleans [1]

"... A January 2006 article in the *Houston Chronicle* titled 'New Orleans Gang Wars Spill into Houston Area,' (cites) ... a criminal such as Ivory 'B-Stupid' Harris, who had been arrested over 19 times, including 2 murder charges, in New Orleans prior to the hurricane, was wanted in Houston for his involvement in several murders in November after the hurricane (Bryant and Khanna, 2006) ... "

The United States Attorney's Office, Eastern District of Louisiana - press release (21 June 2007):

Ivory "B-Stupid" Harris Pleads Guilty in Federal Court [2]

"... Harris and Magee discussed pictures and other information that some of their friends, family, and associates put on the website 'MySpace'. In one of the calls Harris states 'If the feds find the stuff on MySpace, they will convict me of RICO'.

Agents found a 'MySpace Web Site called 'K-UNIT', and obtained numerous pictures, including photos showing Harris holding cash in his hands with the caption "we movin keys and taking over the blocks" and another photo showing Harris, holding a gun and cell phone while wearing a shirt with a picture of (his murder victim) Jermaine Wise that read 'rest in peace'. It was also learned that both Harris and Magee had 'K-Unit' tattoos on their bodies ... "

New Orleans *Times-Picayune* **, 4 October 2007**

Criminal says he's no snitch [3]

"B-Stupid didn't go quietly to prison.

As a federal judge gave him twenty-five years for leaving a trail of violence across New Orleans in 2006—from a killing on Mardi Gras to dealing cocaine and heroin out of a Kenner apartment—the criminal known on the streets as B-Stupid worried about polishing up one fragment of his reputation.

He is no jailhouse snitch.

"... He is mentally disturbed, he has a lack of educational skills', Harris' sister wrote to the court in June.

Keshawn Harris blamed the news media for spreading the word that B-Stupid had agreed to rat out his cohorts.

'Fights have occurred', she wrote. 'Slogans and slants has been thrown. What's the next step, a bloody war'."

A cyberspace memorial

B-Stupid.

Nothing to be said further about the name.

But Ivory "B-Stupid" Harris's sister was obviously proud of her brother, in spite of his being "mentally disturbed." She and his family and friends decided that he deserved a memorial to his accomplishments, and that the web was the place to do it.

Why not?

They built a loving website on MySpace that (among depictions of other significant feats) showed him gloating over the death of Jermaine Wise, one of the men he had recently murdered. Harris was pictured wearing one of the now-standard New Orleans "death notice" RIP memorial t-shirts featuring Wise's picture and name, holding in one hand the phone on which he was informed of his victim's location, and in the other the gun with which he supposedly had ended Wise's life.

It was an advertisement for, and celebration of, murder. On a website called "K-Unit."

I looked for the site this morning, but it seems to have been dismantled, maybe by the FBI who used it to track Harris down and convict him.

He knew the site would "out" him, once he discovered what had happened. But by then it was too late. His admiring relatives had inadvertently given the government all it needed to finally, after almost two dozen attempts, put "B-Stupid" behind bars. The evidence was right there for the Feds, on the K-Unit MySpace, displayed in a relatively attractive web layout format. All they had to do was print it out on heavyweight glossy photo paper and bring hard copies to a judge.

"Twenty-five years," said that judge, who did not believe Harris's "lack of educational skills" was a fitting excuse for multiple murders and uncountable drug-related felonies. To the end "B-Stupid" had no remorse. He was, however, worried that his fellow inmates might think that he had ratted out some of his bloody-handed brethren as part of his plea agreement. "B-Stupid" was smart enough to know the judgment inside the slammer requires no jury, and that execution there in prison requires no closing arguments.

But what was left of his K-Unit memorial?

When I googled "K-Unit+MySpace," all I found was a three-piece semi-punk hair-conscious girl band of that name from Birmingham, England, and, ironically, a thug image-conscious website called mob-staz.com whose front-page feature was a reprinted news story about a young boy who had killed himself over his penis size. In a related story just below, the lead mobsta blogged on how he killed a dog the first time he attempted to drive a car.

Thus goes the web, unregulated in taste, and mostly unhindered by the laws of civilisation. One can only wonder whether the heroically disturbed "B-Stupid" will have internet access in prison [4].

So, his given name, "Ivory," wasn't befitting. Mr Harris decided to be "B-Stupid."

When will you arise?

Sometimes, what seems like randomly chosen nicknames have deep psychic roots, both in themselves and in their method of acquisition. In Louisiana, and especially New Orleans, politicians also seem to have a fondness for such tags. Possibly they think a nickname will render them homier, folksy, more approachable.

There was a statewide election [5] in Louisiana on Saturday 20 October; in listing the candidates (*Times-Picayune*, 14 October 2007) the local newspaper specifies nicknames for forty-seven of what I estimate to be approximately 300 candidates for local office. There is a personal definition set in quotation marks between first and surname in each of those cases.

The handles range from the common ("Tony G," "Spanky," "Vinny," "Buddy") to slightly less familiar ("Snookie," "Zig," "Black," and "Rock"). In one listing in nearby rural St John the Baptist parish,

five out of the first seventeen candidates can be found sporting nicknames ("Lipper," "Dokie," "Bosco," "Casual" and "Netty" , in that
order.)

The election for Louisiana's governorship [6] was won by Piyush "Bobby"
Jindal, the Indian-origin Republican candidate (who adopted his moniker
at the age of 4 from a character in the television series *The Brady
Bunch*). New Orleans's recent mayors include "Moon" Landrieu and
"Dutch" Morial. It is rumoured among the punters that soon, due
to his continuing verbal gaffes, our current mayor may universally be
known via medial quotation marks as Ray "Chocolate City"' Nagin.

I myself, in my own not-so-macho days as an unwilling draftee in this
nation's army, owned a nickname peculiar to that situation. Forty
years ago the vast majority of the American army was composed of
young men like myself, mostly in their late teens or early 20s, who
desperately wanted to forget where they were. Who wanted to forget
that they now had a job where, instead of being fired, they would be
put in jail if they talked back or did an assignment incorrectly. Or, as
a slightly more terminal solution, shot. To that end there was a great
deal of drinking and imbibing of modestly illegal substances. For much
of each day and night, they/we forgot.

While immersed in one such passage of time, my comrades-in-arms (actually my comrades-in-typewriters—we were all clerks, making carbon-
copies on the less dangerous fringes of Asia) and I decided that hence-
forward we would all carry names suitable for comic-book hero-superpowers.
We would be immortal, and as a side-effect, impervious to the rants of
both non-commissioned and junior-grade officers. There was Ant-Man
and Lurch (the giant from *The Addams Family* [7]) and Speed-Man,
and Fly—on and on.

One of the instigators, I was, when it came my turn, at loss for a new,
inventive name. And then it came, out of the dark ether of my brain. I
will never know why this occurred to me just then, but it did. "I'll be
Dead Man," I said,"because nobody can beat a Dead Man. Nobody."
The name stuck.

To this day, I've friends who call or write the Dead Man.

Four decades later I sit musing at these lists of names, all the "Red"
& "Marty" and "Coach" candidates who are asking for the power to
make decisions that will affect the lives of 100,000 fragile and vulnerable
residents of this city.

Then I picture "B-Stupid," who never asked for the power, just took
it, in the process also taking innumerable lives and ruining many more.

He was not alone. During the second weekend of October 2007, the number of people killed [8] in this city rose to 186, topping the 183 murdered in all of 2006, when New Orleans was declared the murder capital of America, with the highest per-capita homicide rate of any major urban city.

It is getting better, please understand. Especially in the repopulated parts of the city. There are the cops on twelve-hour shifts and the national guard [9] and state police and night-sight helicopters, but with all that plus the Feds it still took the authorities here eight years to capture Ivory Harris and put him away. And even then, twenty-five years seems a short time to keep such an unrelentingly dangerous creature in custody. Besides, there another hundred or so other murderers still out there, roaming.

As I look around me every day, I see New Orleanians still trying to act and react based in "normality," moving through their daily lives as if nothing was amiss, making a positive difference, helping each other. This self-giving warmth was the hallmark of the multi-ethnic multicultural civilisation that characterised the city pre-Katrina, and is still central to its character and its people.

We try to ignore the nicknames, whether tagging predators or politicians. We continue to try and interpret the real world as being "normal."

There go those quotation marks again.

Unfortunately, the reality of New Orleans 2007 makes me wonder ever again if even the "Dead Man" would be safe.

URLS

[1] judiciary.house.gov/Oversight.aspx?ID=295
[2] www.usdoj.gov/usao/lae/press/2007/2007_06_21_ivory_b_stupid_harris_plea.htm
[3] www.nola.com/crime/t-p/index.ssf?/base/news-9/119148077671700.xml&coll=1
[4] www.wdsu.com/news/14264903/detail.html
[5] www.nytimes.com/2007/10/22/us/22louisiana.html?hp
[6] www.nytimes.com/2007/10/22/us/22louisiana.html?_r=1&hp&oref=slogin
[7] www.tv.com/addams-family/show/551/summary.html
[8] blog.nola.com/times-picayune/2007/10/woman_shot_to_death_in_eastern.html
[9] www.katc.com/Global/story.asp?S=7228109

Death and life in New Orleans

Within a single day in New Orleans, the passing of two strangers pierces the soul.

Front-pages do not interest me any more. I read the comics, the arts section, the sports news. Then I discard the newspaper, whether it is the *New Orleans Times-Picayune* or the *New York Times*. I know this is selfish, but living where I do, I feel that I have enough grief and confusion in my daily life without absorbing that of others.

Though this Sunday's headlines made me take note. Bold-faced letters atop the page screamed 'five shootings across city'. The most prominent death had occurred close to my home, on a route I drive daily. So I read, as a matter of self-preservation.

A man was assassinated on a busy city street at the wheel of his SUV by three gunmen who boldly pulled alongside in the early afternoon and emptied the clip of an AK-47 assault rifle into the driver. All three gunmen escaped, leaving the weapon and murder vehicle at the scene. The dead man was identified as Glynn Francois, Jr, aged 24.

A front-page colour picture showed a New Orleans police department officer comforting Francois's hysterically grieving sister. The cutline noted 'her white tank-top stained with blood.' She had also been a passenger in the car during the attack.

However, she refused to talk to detectives about the incident on the grounds that police would take up too much of her time. She preferred to 'grieve' on the street corner.

She is now in jail. While she was 'grieving', officers discovered that immediately after the murder she had calmly taken a handgun from her brother's vehicle and stashed it in a nearby convenience store for later use.

I was glad she was sent to jail.

And I was glad her brother was dead.

Forgive me that, please.

24-year-old Francois had over twenty arrests [?] in the last five years, including multiple armed robberies in the university neighbourhood uptown where I teach. Armed robberies in which he would accost young women coming home from the music clubs in the area to take their money and jewellery, first forcing them into alleyways where he would make the women disrobe and then rub his gun over their bodies.

Yet somehow he walked away free in each of his seven trips to the criminal court, and kept slipping through the system, unscathed. Since 2002 he had been arrested again and again, on allegations that included kidnapping, attempted murder, and drug-dealing. In one case he was acquitted of two counts of battery on a police officer, in another he was acquitted of armed robbery.

In 2003 prosecutors dismissed a seven-count indictment against Francois that included sexual battery, armed robbery and kidnapping. He had been released before that trial by putting up a $75,000 cash bond. He had another date in court coming up next month, 13 April, on crack-cocaine charges, though he was roaming around free because he had put up another $10,000 in cash for that bond. He always had large amounts of money to pay for his freedom.

Francois was unemployed.

My Sunday morning was marred by the feeling of satisfaction I felt reading of his demise. I felt dirty with self-righteousness, even though I was reinforced by phone calls from, and conversations with, neighbours and friends. The murder was on everybody's mind. Yes, another of the Bad Guys had been taken out by his own kind, and I could not feel sorry.

So I worked in the yard as penance, hard manual labor clearing last season's banana trees, chopping them up and then hauling the hundreds of pounds of slippery banana trunks and bundled leaves to the kerb for the next day's trash pickup. It was serious work, but a good purgative.

So much so that after a hot bath I felt sufficiently myself to indulge in a late afternoon bicycle run to Tujague's. Tujague's is a Creole bar and restaurant now in business some 152 years, of which I have been privileged to enjoy the last forty. The patrons of this place are a family, generations deeply rooted in the community. People from all walks of life. I had expected a quiet Sunday afternoon cocktail and a conversation or two on Matters of Import.

I walked into a riot. Or what passes for one outside of the Carnival season.

'Twas a funeral. More specifically, the post-funeral wake. A hundred people were laughing, singing, and passing about pictures of themselves and others in costume from Carnival Day. I saw three of myself.

But I could not find out who had died - I also do not read the obituary columns. The closest I came was when a long-time friend said, 'Oh you know, Ronnie.'

'Ronnie?' I inquired.

'Yeah, you know him. Can't believe I don't remember his last name. And I went to the funeral. But he's the dancer.'

'The dancer?'

'Always danced with everybody at every party. Old ladies, little girls, pretty ones, ugly ones. Hell, he even danced with *me*, and I am downright mean with men. Anybody know Ronnie's name?' she shouted.

A young man in overalls at the back of the bar yelled something unintelligible that sounded vaguely like a surname. I knew that the food was laid out in an adjoining room along with pictures of the deceased, and if we had fought our way back there we could undoubtedly have identified the deceased and witnessed his life story in photos, but that would have been a major task, as the place was jammed. The man yelled a name again, but I still couldn't make it out over the roar, and neither could my friend.

We gave up. 'Funny we should be waking him now, as this was his favourite time of the week. He made the Tipitina's *fais do-do* every single Sunday for as long as I can remember', she said.

Tipitina's is a famous local music club in uptown New Orleans, which, for at least the last two decades, has held a traditional Cajun dance every Sunday evening. A free supper comes with an entrance ticket. Even if patrons come as a couple, normally the men and women separate after entry, the men milling about in a section traditionally called *une cage aux chiens* (the dog pen), unless they are dancing. A *fais do-do* [pronounced *FAY-doh-DOH*] is a complete democracy: everybody gets to dance and 'pass a good time'. And dance they do, energetically, giving the party its name. *Fais do-do* [?] means 'make to sleep' in Cajun French. Basically you dance until you drop.

Ronnie, I discovered, had been a legendary dancer, and I vaguely remembered him as a passing blur on a number of occasions. Though I still didn't really know who he was. He never asked me to dance, you see.

The brass band was just arriving as I was leaving. I have to admit that I was already feeling better for having experienced another example of New Orleans's traditional flaunting of the seriousness of Death.

But on my exit I heard the capper.

An elderly couple were having their drinks just outside the door, avoiding the crush, highballs in hand. They were talking about the deceased. I discreetly paused nearby, hoping to finally hear who the person was. After all, I had toasted the man a dozen times already. I should at least know his name.

'Oh I know Ronnie is pissed right now', the man was saying.

I leaned closer.

'I was with him an hour before he passed, you know. Right there in the hospital room. And he was as calm as anybody I ever seen. Asked him if he was OK, was he in pain or anything. Could I maybe do something. And he said no, he was fine, and that he knew he was close to the end, and was not worried one bit. I remember exactly what he said then. 'Neddie', he said, 'Neddie, the only thing I hate about dyin' is that I gotta miss my own damned wake, and I know it's gonna be a doozie.' Smiled at me. An hour later he was dead. Saw his body in the box this morning. He was still smiling.'

I went home then, cured from the horror of the morning, purified from my own dark thoughts. Somehow the wave of positive emotion generated by an anonymous stranger's passing had washed the horror from my soul.

I was forgiven.

In the wake of Ronnie's final *fais do-do*.

Cutting loose

Death and celebration, food and funerals, music and loss—New Orleans holds everything in the same hand. The story of traditional jazzman Pud Brown is a reminder of the city's eternal verities.

After my recent description of the deaths of two strangers, and the effects those occurrences had on my own post-K life, I was reminded by a few New Orleans stalwarts that over a decade ago I had written of another death, also tied to the same location. The occasion was the celebration of the passing life of a close friend, and the few pages I wrote were circulated only to those who knew him.

But I was told this week that his family still keeps their (and my) memory of him alive on a website [1].

I had forgotten the piece, had thought it lost, but I rediscovered "Cutting loose" today, stashed amidst musty electrons and some pictures of my friend. I considered asking your indulgence, but I feel that the story (with minimal updating as it was once part of a *cookbook*), is worth sharing with a wider audience. To me, it once again shows that this town, this wonderful old hole-in-the-wall, holds both a physical and a spiritual place worth saving.

That said, I offer you a story about death, from a cookbook.

Before the afterlife

A New Orleanian would not find it odd that a discussion of living in the city should begin with food and a funeral. Life and death hold each other fondly in these neighbourhoods, two ageless lovers engaging arm and arm to move in a slow sexy tango, bumping and grinding on the dance floor, taking turns leading. Maybe that's why so very few things bother those of us who live here. Different sexual proclivities? Have at it. Unfamiliar racial characteristics? Hey, we all look a little peculiar 'round these parts.

Odd religious identity? Child, only five years ago in the Faubourg Marigny there was an Irish Catholic church, a German Catholic church, a French Catholic church, and a Creole Catholic church, all within a dozen blocks of one another, and all getting along just fine for the last century or so.

Politics? About as vital here as beer-brand preference, which makes it a bit more important than one would wish, but still no big deal. Hellsbells, these folks don't even care what species you are. Dogs would still be in most restaurants if the Feds hadn't sent down so many damned health restrictions. Basically, in this town if you eat the red beans you must be family.

So, dying is not as bad here, they tell me. There's always music. The food is good. And there are cocktails available up to the moment of departure.

I was having just such a beverage in the company of friends when this particular experience with afterlife began. I was at Tujague's, and I myself was quite alive.

Passing through

Tujague's Restaurant holds New Orleans's oldest stand-up bar, the long cypress planking a hangout for off-duty waiters, retired bookies, French Quarter portrait painters, beer truck drivers, writers of all ilk, R&B musicians. And the inevitable tourists.

The bar is comforting and familiar, but the food that emerges from the tiny kitchen lets you know immediately that you're home. I have always believed that there is a singular synapse between the stomach and the soul: the term "gut reaction" seems perfectly descriptive to me. And here in New Orleans the distance between the two seems to shrink. It is readily apparent to residents that the occurrences of daily life and the food consumed during the actual living are directly connected.

At some point I began to write an ongoing narrative, compiling the city's recipes along with my own and flavoring them with events that seem directly connected to the soul—and stomach—of my hometown. The narrative remains unpublished, but the recipes are in daily use in restaurants and my own kitchen.

My original idea was that, to properly appreciate the food, you must digest the place in which it originates.

And thus, Tujague's.

In spite of the extremely limited selection of entrees that are listed daily on the kitchen's blackboard—only the entrée allows choices in its traditional Creole seven-course *table d'hôte* menu—regulars know they can always order the incredibly garlicky—four full heads of garlic used on a huge single bird—*poulet bonne femme*, the only off-the-menu item the kitchen will prepare.

Four people can make a good meal off this huge dish. The solitary consumption of a flavourful "good woman" from Tujague's (the process requires a doggy-bag and two days of additional meals) is one of my few remaining vices, and the possible cause of a recent weight gain. On busy nights, Steve Latter, whose family brought the house back into international prominence in the last twenty-one years of its 152, will only make the dish if you call in a good three hours ahead with your order. Or fifteen minutes if you're a regular. Which I now seem to be.

I first placed my foot on Tujague's brass rail forty-two years ago. That number now seems so extraordinary. On the day after my high-school graduation, I would have never believed I would one day find myself 60 years old, standing in the same place. But sure enough, here I am, looking at a grey-haired, bearded fellow with bags under his eyes and over his belt. He seems a bit defiant, framed in the fourteen-foot-tall reflected universe that runs the entire length of the large room. The mirror that holds this elderly gent was itself brought over in the hold of a sailing ship in 1856 after already gracing a Parisian bistro for ninety years.

Everything in this neighbourhood is old. Vieux Carré does not romantically mean "French Quarter," as so many visitors believe. It means "Old Square." And there I wander, appropriately enough, as old and square as they come.

This building lived an entire life as a Spanish armoury before Guillame Tujague arrived from Mazzeroles, France, to open a restaurant within the two-foot-thick brick and stucco walls. Ceiling fans that once ran off DC electricity are now converted to more modern power, but move just as crankily as they did during Prohibition.

Even the black-and-white tile floor's surface rolls in noticeable grooves like the rising swell of a morning sea, the result of decades of dockworkers, sailors, and butchers making their way to the bar to stand and raise glasses in camaraderie. This is indeed the sovereign "standing" bar of the city. The one large table, available for seating only in the latter part of this century, is made of brass hammered into the shape of a painter's pallet, and is positioned under the room's single unshuttered double window.

Age suits the place, and me, I have decided, generously to us both. The details of setting are important. It's the pleasures inherent in such small matters that make life worth the wretched trouble of passage. Which brings me back to where I started: a particular interconnection of mortality and sustenance.

I was at the Decatur street end of the bar late one particularly hot Tuesday afternoon. My workday had been filled with stops, starts, bobbles and twists, my brain and patience both taken well beyond their natural limits. This is the norm in a business where electrons are manipulated for public gratification.

But my workday was over, it was the happy hour at Tujague's, and Noonie (a direct descendant of the original Guillame) was managing the house.

Jake had just taken over from Mel the day bartender, and was working the cypress, setting up rounds for the beginnings of the evening's crowd, when suddenly the forged iron doors flew open and a female tourist came running in with the phallus of a lens protruding from between her breasts. She paused only to drag in half a breath and ask: "May I [breath] get up on your balcony? [breath] There is a really wonderful [deep breath] parade coming!" She inhaled again and motioned streetward with her neck-strapped 250mm optical tube. Of Oriental origin.

Jake nodded toward his boss, indicating deference to management in such matters. Noonie obligingly moved the woman along, aiming her toward the back staircase and the balcony overlooking the street with a single concise sweep of his own forehead. She went up the steps in quick bounds.

I heard a very active musical wave approaching and looked out to the sound. Near the street's central yellow lines, several friends of mine were walking in step preceding a brass band. Mike Stark, the president of the New Orleans maskmaker's guild, was foremost, directly in front of a pair of trombones. He spotted me through the now open doors of the bar and waved at me to come into the thermal waves of the street and join him.

I hesitated at returning to the heat, but decided to step outside to evaluate the possibility.

It was indeed one more very very hot day in New Orleans.

Two beats, repeat, walk

I am just stepping outside for a look, I told myself again. And immediately found myself pulled into clarinetist Pud Brown's funeral parade. The white handkerchiefs were waving. The umbrellas bouncing. I couldn't resist. I knew Pud had died and I cared about him, even if I had talked myself out of going to the ritual church portion of the service. And I had admired and loved the mourning Mike for years.

Mike Stark, the huge, bald, red-bearded fellow in the caftan, was as much an historic figure in the French Quarter as St Louis cathedral. If Mike needed the comfort of a parade to put Pud away, I would certainly join him, and share the burden. I owed them both that much. I saw Jake the bartender making a concise hand signal as I headed out without a word. Jake understood about such matters.

The procession was Walking to a dirge when I fell into step between Mike and the forward horns of the band. "Just a Closer Walk with Thee" was the tune, and because of the number of veteran paraders involved, the synchronous movement of the group was heartbreakingly beautiful. For those who have not witnessed this death dance, the term "Walk" does not at all describe what happens during the slow tunes in a funeral march. "Just..." right foot steps forward. Pause. "... a closer..." swing the weight forward over the right foot and bring the heel of the left foot up, pointing backwards with the left toes. Pause. "... walk with thee..." left foot forward, even with the right. Pause two beats. Repeat in reverse order.

Once the rhythm asserts itself and the steps become automatic, the Walk is as powerful and emotionally affective a way to move in a group as any ever devised by upright man. The sight of a cortege of this size, a wailing band proceeding a whole block of family, friends and admirers, five or six hundred strong, slowly lifting up, moving forward, and settling back down in front of a creaking horse-drawn catafalque, is hypnotic. The spectacle drives many onlookers, who have no idea of the identity or worth of the departed, to uncontrolled sobbing.

That day tears had been rolling down Mike Stark's face for some time. The small vertical line of salt on each cheek was testament to the fact that he did not care to stop them. I cried, too, even though I knew Pud himself didn't care much for tears, just because of the beauty of the procession and the emotion of the moment. I suppose he would have excused me for that. He'd played hundreds of funerals and normally would be playing his horn up front of the very box that now carried him.

Pud was one of the premiere traditional jazzmen in the Universe. The Universe, by trad standards, may rightly be defined as the twelve-block-by-nine-block area that makes up the French Quarter in New Orleans. Rampart street to the river, Canal to Esplanade. Pud had moved residence not long before his death to be closer to his new musical home at the Palm Court cafe, where he played often and long. He enjoyed having regular, long-term gigs, and never grew bored of the songs he played over and over.

Pud's mouth music

We had met some ten years earlier, when I telephoned him to request his participation in a sunrise set of turn-of-the-century brothel music I was staging. A friendly spirit even to strangers, he asked me over to discuss the gig in person.

Pud was then living on St Peter Street, in one of Tennessee Williams's old habitations. His seven rooms were stacked wall-to-wall and floor to ceiling with music, records, and archaeologically significant instrument parts. It was impossible to see across the width of any of the spaces, and passage was accomplished by moving carefully though blindly through twisting narrow gaps between the tall columns of musical materials. Avalanche was a very real prospect. An unmoving cloud of sparkling particles was suspended in the few shafts of sunlight that pushed their way through the torn and dusty lace curtains at the balcony end of the third-floor apartment. The very air was thick with the music that had been played and the stories that had been told within the walls.

Physically you could tell that Pud had been down a long road, too. His large body sagged and his ruddy face rolled under a shock of white hair, though behind thick glasses his eyes were as lively as a teenager's. He had a smile that would travel through time and space, and make you grin a week later in remembrance.

Pud and I sat on his bed to talk, that being the only clear spot he could offer for seating. The few chairs he had were piled with sheet music to such a height that the top of the heap leaned against the wall near its crown moulding. He slept in the narrow stairwell, on a frayed army cot canopied with an oxygen tent. He wasn't well, even then, and required the pure gas to give him rest. But the space around that thirty-inch-wide bed was full of the happy detritus of a life spent joining harmony, travelling melody, and smiling at the ladies. He had a gentle, quiet voice that somehow lightly carried great weight, very much like the breathy sighing of his horn. He was not worried about the condition of his life or living. Everything was as it was supposed to be.

Nothing much bothered him on the bandstand, either. He made himself comfortable doing the job for which he was born. I found that out when we finally did the "brothel" film shoot, documenting an hour of historic bawdy music from the turn-of-the-century heyday of New Orleans' notorious legal red-light district, Storyville.

Pud had a habit of slipping his false teeth out and hiding them behind his left shoe while he rested between solos. I only noticed the teeth on the floor while in the last throes of post-production editing on the show, and had to go to great lengths to assure that the show aired on American televisions with most of the dental solos removed. In his latter years a patron bought him some better-fitting teeth, but he'd grown accustomed by then to drifting off while the horn wasn't in place between his lips. He'd sit open-mouthed, staring into space, humming the tune while blowing cool air over his gums. Bands learned it was best to keep him busy and the teeth in place.

A high five

Pud Brown was a gentle, caring soul off the stand, and a bearer of the mellow winds of the heart when on. Which accounted for the large turnout at his funeral.

When I joined the parade, pallbearers had already "cut the body loose"—taken the coffin out of the horse-drawn hearse and hefted it in the air three times—in front of the Palm Court to start the parade. This is traditionally done when the cortege passes a spot favored by the deceased.

The bandstand in the Court had definitely been Pud's idea of an earthly heaven.

Now I walked beside Mike the maskmaker in the procession through four long tunes, strutting to the fast numbers and Walking to the slow. The coffin wove its way back and forth through eight blocks of the Quarter, then eastward across Jackson Square in front of the cathedral, until it finally passed though Chartres street one block above Tujague's, on the parade's last leg toward the cemetery. The route allowed me to return to my spot at the bar. And my drink.

Jake, the quintessential New Orleans bartender, had naturally kept my beverage chilled and waiting for me, even though he was unsure of my return. A good thing, too. I'd worked up a sweat, as happens with both temperature and humidity just dropping from the century mark, and not a breath of air stirring. I drank my back of ice water at a gulp, then toasted the departed Pud with a cool but not cold neat whiskey, and thanked him for the afternoon's soul-stirring Walk.

On a sudden whim, I pulled a bill from my pocket and stuffed it into the gaudy maw of the video poker machine that crouched against the wall beside the head of the bar. It was a fiver, but I bet the wad on one hand. As a matter of course I do not gamble, but will infrequently—usually when I am in a pique—put a dollar into one of those machines looking for the reassurance of a crystal ball or horoscope. I want someone, anyone, to tell me definitively if the future is looking good or bad.

So I rather enjoy letting the gaudy metal box sort through its pile of electronic innards and tell me whether I've a positive roll going, or if I should be more on the defensive. I figure that's at least as good a method as consulting the medieval used-car astrological forecast that is carried in almost every otherwise respectable daily newspaper in America. And unlike the machines, the journalists never ever give you your money back. In any case I normally only bet a dollar, not much more than the cost of such a paper.

But on this day a five came out of my pocket, and without hesitation a five went into the machine. I bet the entire amount as a solitary unit of haruspication. It was the right thing to do—spread the entrails of the day and look for a message. I knew that my impulsive behavior was sparked by the emotional energy I had just absorbed from Pud's funeral, and somehow I felt this a necessary finale, or purgative.

Tell me what it means, even if it's bad.

I pressed the "Deal" button. There were four bell-like dings, followed by a great deal of quasi-musical noise.

The screen announced a win of $100 on my investment of five.

It was not my money. I bought the bar a round and a double order of *bon femme* for whomever wished to eat. After tipping Jake, I had my original five dollars left.

Pud was a generous sort, to the very end.

URLS

[1] www.pudbrown.com/

Swimming

"The same water that drowned us, that destroyed our homes,
that poisoned our parks and trees, she gives us this beauty today."
There is poetry amid heartbreak in New Orleans.

"What the hell?"

I am still asleep, dreaming of deep-voiced Sirens moaning from overpowering waters, sound streaming from the murky throat of the Styx.

I am on my way to that other place.

"What?"

No, I am at home, there is a startled cat on my feet, and it is the Mississippi river that runs at the foot of Marigny Street. It is the Mississippi that sounds its low. Sounds it loudly.

Even though the river is three blocks from my home, the slow echoes are strong enough to rattle picture frames and the windows of my bedroom. They sing a long and steady moan, a howl from some primeval soul. Though they are controlled, steady, consistent. I begin to understand.

The orange tabby curls.

I listen. First one, then another.

Now there are many. Five simultaneous singers find a chord and maintain it. It goes on and on. It resonates. A stirring, physically-moving harmony carrying irresistible emotion and inscrutable message.

Yet, I am comforted.

The boat horns were loud enough to wake me, and are gentle enough to put me back to sleep.

And so, I sleep again.

The horns have to be blown, and loudly, when the fog comes in like it has the last three days, because just here the river does its tightest turn, at Algiers Point [1]. A restaurant used to stand on the opposite bank, on that tiny peninsula jutting into the river. You could sit with your cocktails and your meal and for hours watch the giant ocean-going vessels make their way around the point.

It is a masterful dance. The river pilots first power into the turn then suddenly jerk hard to port, the stern sliding all the way around with the bow locked in place mid-river.

Sitting at dinner looking through tall glass French-shuttered windows, the vessels literally pivoted around your table.

It was dizzying. Then, just at a precise moment, the pilot gunned the engines full ahead, to fall instantly again into the deep straight vessel channel as the river passes the Vieux Carré.

It is a frightening manoeuvre in the broad daylight. It is a miraculous combination of engineering and intuition in the dark and fog. And they must stay out of each other's way, these huge moving structures, as long steady lines of ships both come in from, and travel to, the Gulf of Mexico at every hour of the day and night. Through the heart of New Orleans.

Thus this morning's symphonic dirge.

When I finally climb from bed, the slowly evaporating fog has already softened the many ragged post-Katrina [2] edges that remain in the neighbourhood all these months later. An orange glow tints the thick wet blanket of moisture as the sun finds its way slowly to mount slate-armoured rooftops.

This is a rougher place now. True, it is populated by much the same stubborn, ragtag army of carpenters and sculptors, plumbers and painters as before the hurricane. Hell, I live here. But there are new elements, strangers from all over the country, all over the world, walking our streets, looking to cash in on the goldrush of federal money and cheaply-purchased ruined housing.

It is rough, but the Faubourg Marigny has kept itself a simple haven of blue-collar magic and metaphor. This is the neighbourhood where Piety street and Desire street run side-by-side for dozens of blocks, parallel, never meeting, until they come to an end just as they cross Pleasure street.

New Orleans is a city that lives in metaphor.

I am drawn to the levee mid-morning, a short walk, chicory-bitter creamed coffee in hand. A warehouse and dock sits atop the large earthen mound, the water, mimicking the color of my beverage, lapping at its edges. This is the levee that held, and continues to hold, the Mississippi river within its confines. It has my personal confidence and gratitude. My home took no water in the epic of 2005.

There is a spectacle to be seen now that matches the dawn's music. Just offshore the river is topped with a milky, opaque fog a mile long and six to ten feet deep, running completely from east bank to west, brim-full to the top of the high levees. And as I stand there, each of the passing ships makes its maneuver into the turn with its stern swinging broadly, forcing a wide stream of the fog to move toward the east bank where I stand. As it hits the levee it rises, a low-hanging cloud spills over my feet, reaches my waist, and flows down into the neighborhood.

A thick cream off a cappuccino rolls into the streets.

The same water that drowned [3] us, that destroyed our homes, that poisoned our parks and trees, she gives us this beauty today.

I wrote once some years back about the foghorns. I tried to fabricate metred lines, speaking of them like some huge herd of mournful whales, traveling downriver with their echoes, singing to one another as they tried to once again find deep, safe water.

I am now glad to have lost that bit of writing.

Poetry has no place in this city, not for the moment. These are more literal times.

And today, I look at the water and am grateful.

There is nothing else to do, is there?

URLS

[1] www.algierspoint.org/
[2] environment.newscientist.com/channel/earth/hurricane/dn9960
[3] www.hbo.com/docs/programs/whentheleveesbroke/

Windfall

The signs of life in post-Katrina New Orleans are not all human.

Dead, they were all dead.

Spring 2006 was marked in New Orleans by the appearance, in patios and yards everywhere, of thick carpets composed of unmoving migratory butterflies, jewelled dragonflies, moths and honeybees.

Jim Gabour is an award-winning film producer, writer and director, whose work focuses primarily on music and the diversity of cultures. He lives in New Orleans, where he is artist-in-residence and professor of video technology at Loyola University.

In its zeal to stifle the clouds of aggressive disease-riddled carrion-flies and mosquitoes, the government (which government, we don't know, as they all seem to have dominion over New Orleans these days) had adopted wholesale night-time aerosol-bombing from crop-dusting planes and daytime fogging from truck-mounted fumigators. Residents appreciated the reduction of biting insects, but simultaneously mourned the quick loss of the first gay fluttering colors seen in the city in months. More seriously, for those of us who grow things, was the sudden removal of pollinators for flowering trees and plants.

Backyard fruit-and-vegetable crops never had a chance that spring.

The natural predators of the insects, the myriad of lizards and frogs native to our swampy city, were also in large part destroyed by the insecticides.

Those of us who took pride in growing a portion of our own food, and doted on the simple beauty of our environment, once again felt betrayed, on yet another level.

The living city

Eighteen months later we are recuperating. This autumn the butterflies came back, the bees buzzed about, and the first few baby frogs appeared around the fringes of backyard fountains and ponds.

Frogs! Who would believe that I would care about frogs? But these are no common amphibians. Hyla avivoca, The Bird-voiced Treefrog, is native to New Orleans, and in recent years state legislators with no better things to do (this hurricane-recovery business having become tiresome) have officially crowned avivoca as "The State Frog". I have no idea what responsibility that title carries, and it seems neither do the frogs, as I have seen no tadpoles bearing gilded inscriptions, nor hopping amphibians beribboned with multi-coloured medals to denote their governmental distinction. At least not yet.

It wouldn't be a complete surprise if the legislature—back in session— held a week's debate on which month should hold State Frog Day. Dealing with the city's recovery is boring hard work, after all. The state already has a Frog Festival, the thirty-fifth version of which was just celebrated three months ago, over in Cajun territory in Rayne, Louisiana. Cajuns don't use the proper Parisian grenouille to desig- nate their honouree, however. Their word for these large bullfrogs is probably the best onomatopoeia I have ever heard: ouaouaron, pro- nounced wah-wah-ROHN. Tell me that doesn't instantly say frog.

Though the diminutive "state" Bird-voiced Treefrogs lack their own individual festival, this has not deterred the returning avivoca from their passion, and every night now that the weather has turned cooler and windows are open, the neighborhood drops into sleep to the sweet song and warbles of these talented creatures.

They also eat at night, the frogs, and mosquitoes are slowly disap- pearing. Of course the singers have been assisted in reducing the blood-sucking insect population by the reemergence of their tailed kin. Chameleons and geckos, salamanders and newts, with spots and stripes and neon colors have joined forces and now fill every shady spot under every bush and structure on the block. They preen and strut and eat the bad guys.

Another totally new addition to the flora of the Faubourg Marigny neighborhood since Katrina are dozens upon dozens of huge "volunteer" papaya trees, each bearing hundreds of pounds of delectable fruit. They are in every yard. I have heard speculation that the ultimate source was a single tree nurtured by a family near the late, lamented El Palaceo bodega. Though the Cubano family did not return after the storm, their tree and its fruit and seeds were ripped apart by the wind and spread over a dozen square blocks. This year we are reaping the bounty, and with the resurgent and always abundant native banana plants, we are again eating well from our yards.

In another ironic bit of flora recovery, the "Resurrection" ferns are back. These amazing resilient plants primarily inhabit the limbs of the Live Oak trees that were so badly damaged in Katrina. In their dormant state, when the ferns are stressed, they dry so completely as to be completely invisible, existing as a part of the grey scaly bark of the oaks. When they have the right living conditions, overnight they find a way to come back to life, and coat the trees in a lush green blanket. As they have this past week.

On the fauna side, once-domestic animals, pets abandoned in the face of the evacuation, often on the legally-binding orders of the soldiers and police officers who stripped pets from evacuees boarding buses out of the City, have also begun to re-approach humans.

For the last four months, three black cats have co-inhabited our back-yard. We don't know if they are from the same feral litter, but feed them morning and night, and each day they have come closer and acted friendlier.

One, a tuxedo whom some call Blackie and I call Foots (he has white spats) now comes to me and will even sit in my lap. He was obviously captured after the storm, castrated and released, as is evidenced by his left ear, which is missing its top third. Force-fixed cats were caught and disfigured in that manner immediately post-Katrina, when every animal was considered feral, rabid and dangerous. The missing ear was to prevent their being picked up again. At least they were not eutha-nized, which was the case with many of the personal pets confiscated at the Katrina bus boarding sites.

The three cats are often joined at breakfast and dinner by a large raccoon who has taken up residence in the abandoned fire-station on the back of the block. We thought him a lone straggler these last months and have watched him grow ever larger, until just the other morning when he arrived for breakfast with two short and fuzzy versions of himself.

The three masked stripers love the papayas and bananas that fill their dish each morning.

The fact that the fruits are once again homegrown does not impress them.

In the wings

One less-positive sign that the effects of our urban trauma have not yet left, however, is an almost metaphorical physical apparition.

It involves parking.

Some years ago, on Loyola Avenue downtown near City Hall, a group of disciplined and creative artists created a multi-storied trompe l'oeil painting of a clarinet. It is quite beautiful, and from a distance looks like... a multi-storied clarinet. The painters even made the reflections in the chrome of the instrument match the buildings and area around it. Unfortunately, a part of that view is a quite banal asphalt parking-lot.

That lot, immediately below the clarinet, has somehow been chosen as the official encampment of the Louisiana national guard, and though they are thankfully not part of the reflection, at the mouthpiece of the instrument sit dozens of desert-camouflaged, bullet-proof military Humvees. And dozens more military police cars.

All of which daily drive our streets.

Amidst the returning butterflies.

Resources

A brief guide to suggested websites, institutes and books for further research, reading, study and engagement about climate change, hurricanes... and New Orleans

Websites

- Jim Gabour
  www.jimgabour.com/

- Terence Blanchard
  www.terenceblanchard.com/

- chinadialogue
  www.chinadialogue.net

- Environmental News Network
  www.enn.com/

- Greater New Orleans Community Data Center
  www.gnocdc.org/

- Grist
  www.grist.org/

- Kyoto2.org
  www.kyoto2.org/

- Louisiana State University—hurricane research
  www.lamer.lsu.edu/resources/hurricanes.htm

- National Hurricane Center
  www.nhc.noaa.gov/

- New Orleans
  www.nola.com/

- New Orleans Hurricane Center
  www.nola.com/hurricane/

- New Scientist—climate change
  environment.newscientist.com/channel/earth/climate-change/

- Planet Ark
  www.planetark.org/

- RealClimate
  www.realclimate.org/

- SciDevNet
  www.scidev.net/dossiers/index.cfm?fuseaction=dossierItem&Dossier=4

- World view of global warming—photography
  www.worldviewofglobalwarming.org/

- Yale Forum—climate change and the media
  yaleclimatemediaforum.org/

Institutes

- American Association for the Advancement of Science (AAAS)—climate change
  www.aaas.org/news/press_room/climate_change/

- E3G
  www.e3g.org/index.php

- Intergovernmental Panel on Climate Change
  www.ipcc.ch/

- International Institute of Environment and Development (IIED)—climate change
  www.iied.org/CC/index.html

- The Royal Society—climate change
  www.royalsoc.ac.uk/landing.asp?id=1278

- Sustainability
  www.sustainability.com/

- Tyndall Centre for Climate Change Research
  www.tyndall.ac.uk/

Books

- Kirstin Dow & Thomas E Downing, *The Atlas of Climate Change* (Earthscan, 2006)
  `shop.earthscan.co.uk/ProductDetails/mcs/ProductID/838/GroupID/`
  `4/CategoryID/6/v/d7fe3ac8-7053-48cb-a0ff-66f266291536`

- Tim Flannery, *The Weather Makers* (Atlantic Monthly Press, 2006) US, UK
  `www.groveatlantic.com/grove/bin/wc.dll?groveproc~genauth~1497`

- Robert Henson, *The Rough Guide to Climate Change* (Rough Guides, 2006)
  `www.roughguides.com/website/shop/products/Climate-Change.aspx`

- Elizabeth Kolbert, *Field Notes From a Catastrophe* (Bloomsbury, 2006)
  `www.bloomsburyusa.com/catalogue/details2.asp?isbn=9781596911253`

- Louise McKinney, *New Orleans: A Cultural History* (Oxford University Press, 2007)
  `www.us.oup.com/us/catalog/general/subject/HistoryAmerican/Southern/`
  `~~/dmlldz11c2EmY2k9OTc4MDE5NTMwMTM2Ng==`

- Hans Joachim Schellnhuber et al, eds., *Avoiding Dangerous Climate Change* (Cambridge University Press, 2006)
  `www.cambridge.org/uk/catalogue/catalogue.asp?isbn=0521864712`

- David Shearman & Joseph Wayne Smith, *The Climate Change Challenge and the Failure of Democracy* (Praeger, 2007)
  `www.greenwood.com/catalog/C34504.aspx`

openDemocracy articles

- **openDemocracy** writers examine the fallout of the hurricane Katrina disaster.
  `news.bbc.co.uk/1/hi/in_depth/americas/2005/hurricane_katrina/`
  `default.stm`

- Ian Christie, "When the levee breaks" (2 September 2005)
  `www.opendemocracy.net/globalization-climate_change_debate/levee_`
  `2801.jsp`

- Sidney Blumenthal, "A pattern of calamity: 9/11, Katrina, Iraq" (5 September 2005)
  www.opendemocracy.net/democracy/calamity_3881.jsp

- Terry Lynn Karl, "Bush's second Gulf disaster" (6 September 2005)
  www.opendemocracy.net/globalization-climate_change_debate/gulf_disaster_2808.jsp

- Andrei Codrescu, "New Orleans or Baghdad?" (6 September 2005)
  www.opendemocracy.net/globalization-climate_change_debate/other_2809.jsp

- Michel Thieren, "Katrina's triple failure: technical, ethical, political" (6 September 2005)
  www.opendemocracy.net/globalization-climate_change_debate/lessons_2811.jsp

- Maggie Lee, "Grenada's ill wind" (21 September 2005)
  www.opendemocracy.net/globalization-climate_change_debate/grenada_2857.jsp

- Sidney Blumenthal, "Bush's Potemkin village presidency" (22 September 2005)
  www.opendemocracy.net/democracy/bush_2861.jsp

Authors

Jim Gabour

Artist in Residence and Professor of Video Technology

Jim Gabour is an award-winning film/video producer and director, whose work focuses primarily on music and the diversity of cultures. He holds a Master of Fine Arts degree from Louisiana State University. During his career, he has earned five Cable ACE Awards and medals at the International Film & Television Festival of New York and the WorldFest Film Festival. In both 2001 and 2004 Gabour was the featured director of the year at the International Broadcasters Conference in Amsterdam.

In 2002 he produced and directed multi-Grammy-Award-winner Norah Jones' concert long-form for Capitol and Blue Note Records. The resulting multi-platinum DVD spent five weeks at #1 in worldwide sales. Recent projects include a live DVD with hiphop duo Floetry in 2003, NARAS' musical *Heroes* awards and a second Norah Jones DVD in 2004, and a documentary on famed soul singer Al Green in 2005. Gabour's feature-length documentary film *Flow: Living in the Stream of Music* was released in Fall 2006, and the film's DVD was nominated for a 2007 Grammy as *Best Longform Music Video*.

Gabour is a member of the National Academy of Recording Arts and Sciences, National Academy of Television Arts and Sciences, National Academy of Cable Programming, International Film & Television Festival, and the International Broadcasters Conference. He has been with the College of Music faculty since 2005.

Office phone: 504-865-3984

E-mail: jgabour@loyno.edu

Website: www.jimgabour.com

Terence Blanchard

Terence Blanchard is an award-winning trumpeter and composer. He has scored over forty major films. He and Jim Gabour were nominated for a 2007 Grammy for their film Flow: Living in the Stream of Music. Terence has been nominated for two more 2008 Grammy awards for his latest album, A Tale of God's Will: Requiem for Katrina. His website is `www.terenceblanchard.com/`

www.ingramcontent.com/pod-product-compliance
Lightning Source LLC
Chambersburg PA
CBHW031512270326
41930CB00006B/374